Murus ille famosus

Murus ille famosus

(that famous wall)

Depictions and Descriptions
of Hadrian's Wall before Camden

By
WILLIAM D. SHANNON

CUMBERLAND AND WESTMORLAND
ANTIQUARIAN AND ARCHAEOLOGICAL SOCIETY
Tract Series Vol. XXII

Cumberland and Westmorland
Antiquarian & Archaeological Society

C&W TRACT SERIES No. XXII

Hon. General Editor
Dr Jean Turnbull

© William D. Shannon

ISBN 978 1 873124 45 1

Published 2007

Printed by
Titus Wilson & Son, Kendal
2007

Cover:
Matthew Paris 'A', c.1250: British Library, Cotton Ms, Claudius D.VI, fol. 12v.
Reproduced by permission of the British Library.

ACKNOWLEDGEMENTS

I would like to thank Ben Edwards for his help and encouragement in numerous discussions before, during and after the first draft, and for our collaboration on our joint article of 2001, without which the current work would never have been contemplated. I would also like to thank Dr Mike Winstanley for reading and commenting one of the early drafts, before it was sent off to the referees. This final version owes a huge debt to Professor David Shotter and Dr John Todd, who made a significant contribution to the evolution of the piece by their positive criticism. In particular I would to thank Professor Shotter for his valuable pointers with regard to 'Spartianus': and to Dr Todd for checking my Latin, meticulously checking and updating some of my references, and drawing my attention to the use of the Wall as a medieval boundary marker. Finally, I would like to thank the editor, Dr Jean Turnbull, for her patience and attention to detail. Responsibility for the opinions expressed, for the conclusions, and for any remaining errors, rests with me.

LIST OF ILLUSTRATIONS

Murus ille famosus
Depictions and Descriptions of
Hadrian's Wall before Camden[1]

Eric Birley, in his *Research on Hadrian's Wall* distinguished between, on the one hand, the 'ancient literary sources' amongst whom he included Bede, and on the other hand the Antiquaries beginning with Camden, 'the first author to deal with the Wall at length in print'.[2] This is not to say Birley ignored all authors between Bede and Camden: indeed, he acknowledged the debt owed by Camden in the first edition of *Britannia* to the authors of three earlier manuscripts. The first of these was Leland, who had visited *the Picth Waulle* in *c*.1539, and whose *Itinerary* not only contained a list of places along the Wall provided to him by one Doctor Davel, but also included what Birley called the 'primary references to the Wall's ditch and to the Vallum'.[3] Secondly, Birley mentions a letter of *c*.1572, by Christopher Ridley, curate of Haltwhistle, which was first published in 1827 by John Hodgson in his *History of Northumberland*, and refers to the *wall builded betwixt the Brittons & Pightes*.[4] This letter had given Camden the famous story of the brass speaking-tube alleged to run the length of the Wall, and also contained what has hitherto been regarded as the first mention of milecastles.[5] The third of Camden's sources was an anonymous manuscript of 1574 which described *Hadrians wall*, based on notes the writer made following a visit to Edward Threlkeld, Chancellor of Hereford, born at Burgh-by-Sands. The author of this manuscript was identified by M. A. Richardson in *Newcastle Tracts* of 1849 as Sampson Erdeswicke, although Birley states that this identification is unlikely. In addition to these sources

---

[1] The quotation comes from Ranulph Hidgen, who wrote in *c*.1320 of *Vallum Severi sive murus ille famosus*: 'The wall of Severus, or that famous wall': C. Babington & J. R. Lumby (eds.), *Polychronicon Ranulphi Higden Monachi Cestriensis*, London, Rolls Series, I, 1865-6, 66.

[2] E. Birley, *Research on Hadrian's Wall* (Kendal, 1961), 1.

[3] L. Toulmin Smith (ed.), *The Itinerary of John Leland in or about the years 1535-1543* (1st edn. 1907, reprinted London, 1964), 5 (Part IX), 60-61: Birley, 2.

[4] Birley, 2-4.

[5] 'At every mylis end theyr hath been a great bildyng or castle having thre curtyngis', quoted in Birley, 3.

for the first edition of *Britannia*, Birley also named other northern antiquaries contacted by Camden on his visit to the Wall in 1599, and whose information was incorporated into the later editions of *Britannia*, notably Reginald Bainbrigg, master of Appleby School.

In some respects, Birley was re-treading the path of R. G. Collingwood in his *History of the Problem* (1921), who had divided the early sources into three, 'The Ancient Authorities' (the *Antonine Itinerary*, the *Augustan History*, Eutropius, Orosius, Eusebius, Cassiodorus and the like), 'The Native Historians' (Gildas, Bede and Nennius) and 'The Period of Surface Inspection' (Ridley, Camden and later visitors).[6] In his article, Collingwood had in fact gone well beyond the earlier account to be found in Hodgkin's *Literary History of the Wall* (1896), which had ended with Bede, the author announcing that he had decided not to address the 'thorny questions ... connected with the terrible name of Nennius'.[7] However, neither Collingwood, nor Birley, would have disagreed too strongly with the assertion of an American geographer, Haynes, who wrote in 1890 that

The oldest writer who gives its dimensions is the Venerable Bede ... The next eyewitness comes eight hundred and fifty years later.[8]

More than 100 years after Haynes, the fourteenth edition of the *Handbook to the Roman Wall* (2006), the most recently published account of the Wall, similarly has no-one filling this 800 year gap between Bede and the above listed antiquaries: and the same can be said of every earlier edition of the *Handbook*, going right back to Collingwood Bruce's *Wallet Book*.[9] Indeed it appears to be true of almost every writer who has ever touched upon the historiography of the Wall.

In fact, though, it is unlikely that there was any time during those intervening years when there was no knowledge of the Wall. Unsurprisingly, those living in the vicinity of the Wall were very much aware of its presence, and routinely used it in describing or defining parts of their boundaries. Thus the Lanercost *Cartulary* contains numerous

---

[6] R. G. Collingwood, 'Hadrian's Wall: A History of the Problem', *Journal of Roman Studies*, **11**, 1921, 37-66.

[7] T. Hodgkin, 'The Literary History of the Roman Wall', *Archaeologia Aeliana*, 2nd series, **XVIII**, 1896, 83-108.

[8] H. W. Haynes, 'The Roman Wall in Britain', *Journal of the American Geographical Society of New York* **22**, 1890, 157-210. The 'eyewitness' reference is to Christopher Ridley.

[9] D. J Breeze, *J. Collingwood Bruce's Handbook to the Roman Wall, Fourteenth Edition* (Newcastle upon Tyne, 2006).

references from *c.*1165 to the end of the thirteenth century to the *murus,* usually qualified by either *antiquus* or *vetus* (ancient, old), while the Wetheral *Cartulary* has one reference of *c.*1200 to the *antiquum fossatum* and *murum.*[10] Whitworth has given other examples, some later, but also including a twelfth-century Hexham charter which mentions the *muri romanorum* ('the wall of the Romans').[11]

However, medieval knowledge of the Wall was much more widespread than merely amongst the adjacent land-owners. References to the Wall in the chronicles regularly occur: and with the coming of printing such accounts became even more widely available. Admittedly, most were largely repetitions or reinterpretations of traditional accounts derived from 'the native historians': but some authors appear to have added occasional details based upon their own or others' observations. Moreover, it has long been known amongst cartographic historians that certain medieval manuscript maps and early-modern printed maps had also depicted the Wall, thereby demonstrating a general awareness of the Wall as an exceptional feature of the English landscape, while at the same time possibly contributing to increasing that awareness, and spreading it beyond these shores.

It is the contention of this paper that the Roman Wall never disappeared from view in the way that many of its historians seem to have believed: instead, it remained in the forefront of educated national consciousness. Indeed, the medieval writer Ranulph Higden could call it *murus ille famosus,* in the confident expectation that his readers would be well aware of its fame: while later writers, and possibly cartographers too, may have come to see it as very much a *national* monument, making a contribution to growing ideas of nation amongst the English, and perhaps amongst the Scots too.[12]

---

[10] I am most grateful to Dr John Todd for these references. J. Todd (ed.) *Lanercost Cartulary,* Surtees Society, **CCIII**, and CWAAS Record Series **XI**, 1997, nos. 1, 43, 58, 97, 98, 140, 144, 189, 190, 201, 206, 225, 256, 277. J. E. Prescott, *The Register of the Priory of Wetherhal,* CWAAS Record Series 1, 1897, 225.

[11] A. M. Whitworth, *Hadrian's Wall: Some aspects of its Post-Roman Influence on the Landscape,* BAR British Series, **296**, 2000, 41-44.

[12] 'that famous wall': Ranulph Higden, *c.*1320: Babington, *Polychronicon Ranulphi,* **I**, 66. Bede had also called it '*murum ... famosum atque conspicuum*' ('this famous and remarkable wall'): see B. Colgrave & R. A. B. Mynors, *Bede's Ecclesiastical History of the English People* (Oxford, 1969), 44-5: L. Sherley-Price, *Bede: A History of the English Church and People* (Harmondsworth, 1965), 52. Camden used very similar words *Murus ille celeberrimus,* William Camden, *Britannia,* 1587 edn., 532.

The 'native historians'

Collingwood's three 'native historians', Gildas, Bede and Nennius were without doubt the source of nearly everything that was to be written throughout the middle ages about the two walls which crossed Britain: it is worth therefore rehearsing in some detail what they had to say. First, Gildas, said to be a native of Clydeside, wrote around A.D. 540 a very brief account of two walls, for which there is no obvious classical source. He described a poor-quality wall (*murus*), mainly of turf, which by implication, although not stated as such, appears to be the northern one, which we now call the Antonine. Gildas also wrote of a slightly later proper stone wall (again *murus*), which ran straight from sea to sea and which appears to be the one we now call Hadrian's.[13] The construction of both of these were dated by Gildas to the very end of the Roman occupation, as indeed was the series of towers he reported as having been built along the south coast of Britain at the same time as the second wall.

Bede, living in Jarrow, completed his *History* in A.D. 731, in which he provided what Collingwood called 'the first complete Mural theory'.[14] Like Gildas, Bede regarded the construction of the northern turf wall as being associated with the end of the Empire: but, as R. G. Collingwood pointed out, Bede's account is in part an unattributed and expanded quotation from Orosius.[15] In Bede's version, the southern barrier was constructed in two stages, first under Severus as a turf rampart (*vallum*) with ditch (*fossa*), fortified with a series of towers.[16] Subsequently according to Bede, this time quoting Gildas, the complex was rebuilt as a strong wall of stone, at a date which Bede placed immediately after the instruction sent by the Romans to the Britons, ordering them to look to their own

[13] M. Winterbottom (ed. & trans.), *Gildas, The Ruin of Britain and other works* (London, 1978), 149. Because of the range of terminology used by the various sources, unless the author concerned names them otherwise, the terms 'northern wall' and 'southern wall' will be used for what we now call the Antonine Wall and Hadrian's Wall respectively.

[14] Collingwood, *History of the Problem*, 47.

[15] Collingwood, *History of the Problem*, 46. The original quotation, from Orosius, **vii**, 17, can be found in R. W. Moore (ed.), *The Romans in Britain: A Selection of Latin Texts with a Commentary* (London, 3rd edn. 1954, reprinted 1968), 82.

[16] Although *vallum* strictly meant palisade, Bede's description makes it is clear he is talking of an earthwork, made of turf, fronted by a ditch and surmounted by a palisade. See Hodgkin, 108 & Sherley-Price, 43.

defence.[17] Bede, of course, was not to know that present day scholars would now generally regard this famous 'rescript of Honorius', reported by Zosimus, not as referring to the towns of the Britons as Bede had thought, but instead as being addressed to the towns of Bruttium in Southern Italy.[18]

Bede, however, went on to provide apparent eye-witness accounts of both walls, saying of the northern one that 'the remains of this extensive earthwork can be clearly seen to this day', extending from *Peanfahel* or *Penneltun* (= Kinneil, near Falkirk) to the city of *Alcluith* (= Dumbarton, on the Clyde). Separately, he reported of the southern wall that it was 'eight foot in breadth, and twelve foot in height; and, as can be seen, ran straight from east to west'.[19]

The next 'native historian', Nennius, writing around A.D. 796 or soon after, although not as an eyewitness, added some new detail but at the same time contributed considerable confusion to the story. In the Nennius version there were two walls, both built to keep the Picts and the Irish from the Britons, but built by two different men, both called Severus.[20] Taking his account according to Collingwood in part from Bede and in part from Eusebius, but adding original information too, he wrote of a wall and embankment (*murus et agger*), built by Severus and called *Guaul* in the British language, which ran for 132 miles. Both Eusebius and Orosius had used this mileage figure, the former copying the latter: however, Bede had not quoted it, presumably because from his local knowledge he knew it to be wrong.[21] Unfortunately, Nennius said that this first wall ran from *Penguaul* (*Cenail* in Scots, *Peneltun* in English) to the estuary of the Clyde, using the same places Bede had used for the later, northern wall.

Nennius added that this Severan wall was later rebuilt under Carausius, and was fortified with seven towers: he then went on to give an account of 'the second Severus' (*secundo etiam Severo*), who, after the time of Maximian, built another wall, this one from *Tinemuthe* (Tynemouth) to *Boggenes* (Bowness).[22]

---

[17] Sherley-Price, 52.

[18] D. Mattingly, *An Imperial Possession, Britain in the Roman Empire 54 B.C.-A.D. 409* (London, 2006), 530.

[19] Sherley-Price, 52.

[20] J. Morris (ed. & trans.), *Nennius: British History and the Welsh Annals* (London, 1980), 11, 23, 52, 64. *Guaul* derives from the Latin *Vallum*, a palisade or rampart.

[21] For Orosius' account see Hodgkin, 107.

[22] Morris, *Nennius*, 11, 52.

The medieval chroniclers

The chroniclers who followed were faced with the problem of reconciling these disparate accounts and there was a tendency for them to do so by assuming there was but one Wall, the southern one. Both the Winchester and Peterborough versions of the Anglo-Saxon Chronicle merely refer to one wall-building episode, between A.D. 189 and 202 when Severus built a rampart (A-S *dice*) with palisade from sea to sea.[23] However, the Chronicle of Æthelweard (d.1002), called this feature the Severan *fossa* (which was translated by Philemon Holland as 'a ditch or trenche').[24] Despite adding that behind this feature was built a wall with turrets (*murus … cum turribus*), Æthelweard's emphasis on the *ditch* rather than the *wall* was to rebound down the years, as will be shown later.

Amongst the three broadly contemporary post-Conquest chroniclers, Geoffrey of Monmouth was the most influential, either creating or first publicising the Brutus story in 1136, which 'provided the people of Britain with their origin myth'.[25] Although he claimed his prime source was 'a certain very ancient book written in the British language', so far as his account of the Wall is concerned Geoffrey seems mainly to have used Bede and Gildas to produce a coherent account of a single barrier across Britain, built in two stages. The first stage was under Severus, when a rampart was constructed 'between Deira and Albany'. Subsequently, as a last act before the Romans withdrew, the Wall itself was built.[26]

The first part of Henry of Huntingdon's chronicle appeared at almost the same time as Geoffrey's, *c*.1133.[27] Henry mentions Eutropius (fl. *c*.370) as a source, but his account of the Severan rampart is taken straight from Bede.[28] Later, in Henry's version as in

---

[23] M. Swanton (ed. & trans.), *The Anglo-Saxon Chronicle* (London, 1996), 8-10. The Anglo-Saxon Chronicle uses the word *dice* for this feature, which could mean either 'ditch' or' rampart'.

[24] A. Campbell (ed. & trans.), *The Chronicle of Æthelweard* (Edinburgh, 1962). The version consulted, which would have been available to Camden for the later editions, was *Chronicorum Ethelwerdi Libri IIII* (London, 1596). See also Camden, 1637 edn., trans. P. Holland, 791.

[25] C. Given-Wilson, *Chronicles: The Writing of History in Medieval England* (London, 2004), 4.

[26] L. Thorpe (ed. & trans.), *Geoffrey of Monmouth: The History of the Kings of Britain* (London, 1966), 126, 144.

[27] D. Greenway (ed. & trans.), *Henry, Archdeacon of Huntingdon, Historia Anglorum: The History of the English People* (Oxford, 1996), lxi.

[28] Greenway, 50-51.

6

Geoffrey's, shortly before the Romans withdrew, the Britons are instructed to build a wall '*super uallum Seueri*', which Forester translated as 'on the ramparts of Severus', although Greenway's more recent translation has 'beyond the rampart'.[29] Henry added that 'the remains of that very wide and high rampart may be seen to this day': it is possible that this is a contemporary eyewitness account, but it is more likely to be no more than a paraphrase of Bede.[30]

There is some doubt, arising from the use of that word *super*, as to whether Henry meant one wall built upon another, two walls in close proximity – or two walls at some distance from one another. The most likely reading of these three is that Henry, like Geoffrey, assumed there was a single wall site, by implication the southern one. Unfortunately, basing his description on Bede, he then says that this wall extended from *Peneltune* to the city of *Aldclyhit*, thus giving later historians such as Ranulph Higden the problem of identifying those places along the line of the southern wall instead of, as Bede meant them to be, on the northern.

Writing in the years up to 1126, and revised *c*.1135, the third great chronicler, William of Malmesbury, had little to say about the period before the coming of the Saxons, but nevertheless he gave a passing mention to 'the famous rampart, of which everyone has heard, from sea to sea', built by Severus.[31] William also referred to the plan to build a later wall before the Romans finally withdrew.[32]

Over the next 500 years, these accounts were recycled and plagiarised, especially so in the case of Geoffrey of Monmouth's account, which was the prime source for the popular *Brut* stories.[33] However, a little new information did appear in the thirteenth century, in the *Flores Historiarum*, for many years attributed to 'Matthew of Westminster', or Matthew Paris, but now attributed to Roger of Wendover and others. The account in the *Flores*, of Severus

[29] Greenway, 70-71: T. Forester (ed. & trans.), *The Chronicle of Henry of Huntingdon* (First published 1853, facsimile reprint Felinfach, 1991), 33.

[30] Greenway, 70-71.

[31] '*celebrem illam et uulgatissimam fossam de mari ad mare duxit*' R. A. B. Mynors, R. M. Thomson & M. Winterbottom (ed. & trans.), *William of Malmesbury: Gesta Regum Anglorum, History of the English Kings* (Oxford, 1998), I, xxii-xxiii & 16-17.

[32] Mynors, *William of Malmesbury*, 18-21.

[33] 186 Latin manuscripts of Geoffrey are still extant, not counting the numerous vernacular *Bruts* in Welsh and French (Thorpe, 28-9). See also P. Roberts (trans.), *The Chronicle of the Kings of Britain Translated from the Welsh copy attributed to Tysili* (First published London, 1811: facsimile reprint, Felinfach, 2000).

constructing 'a great ditch and wall' (*fossatum magnum murumque*) seems to have been taken from Gildas, Bede and Nennius, or possibly even directly from Orosius, as the *Flores* gave its length as 132 miles: however, the added original touch was specifically to date the Severan building works to the year A.D. 205. The second phase, the turf wall, is dated to A.D. 420, and its final rebuilding in stone to A.D. 421.[34]

The next significant original chronicler was Ranulph Higden of Chester, a hugely influential writer whose *Polychronicon*, written in the 1320s, was translated into English by John Trevisa in the 1380s, and became one of the first books in English to be printed by Caxton, in 1482.[35] Hidgen used Gildas, Bede, and Nennius as well as the above chroniclers, together with Eutropius, Cassiodorus, Orosius, Eusebius and many other sources. Higden again assumed just the one wall (*vallum*), built by Severus, but he gave its length as 122 miles, rather than 132.[36] The section in which he does so follows one in which he quotes from Eusebius, so this is probably a copying error from that source. Higden then goes on to quote from Bede on the Wall's construction by Severus, after which he tries to reconcile its location by concluding that *Alcuid* must be 'not very far from Carlisle' although he says others would locate it at Aldborough on the Ouse, or at Brougham on the Eden.[37]

Higden normally quoted his sources at the beginning of each section: but before comments for which he is the sole authority he instead tended to put his own name, *Ranulphus*. It is therefore interesting to note that he did this before another reference to Carlisle, in which he reported that 'that city has within it some part of that famous wall that crosses Northumberland'.[38] Although Higden is known to have travelled through Cheshire, Lancashire, Shropshire and Derbyshire, there is no evidence of any visit further

---

[34] *Flores Historiarum per Matthaeum Westmonasteriensis* (London, 1570) (Early English Books On-Line), 114, 146-7. The word *fossatum* is not classical Latin, but can be found in R. E. Latham, *Revised Medieval Latin Word-List* (Oxford, 1965). See also H. O. Core (ed.), *Rogeri de Wendover Chronica sive Flores Historiarum*, London, English Historical Society, **I**, 1841-5.

[35] C. Babington (ed.), *Polychronicon Ranulphi Higden Monachi Cestriensis* (London, 1865), **I**, lxi-lxvii.

[36] *vallum in Britannia per centum viginti duo passuum millia a mare usque ad mare deducens.* *Polychronicon*, Lib. IV (Babington, **V**, 42).

[37] *non multum distet a Lugubalia id est Caerliel*: Babington, **II**, 66,

[38] *Habetque haec urbs in se aliquam partem illius famosi muri qui transcindit Northimbria*, Babington, **II**, 68.

north: yet the language used here sounds very much like personal experience, particularly when taken in association with another note of his, to the effect that Hexham is close to the Wall.[39] Most educated Englishmen in the fifteenth and well into the sixteenth century would have been familiar with the *Polychronicon*, particularly in the Trevisa translations and via the Caxton and Wynken de Worde printed editions.[40] However, the success of the *Brut* showed there was also a demand for more popular works than the learned *Polychronicon*. One author who bridged the gap between the popular and the scholarly was John Hardyng, whose verse chronicle was first presented to Henry VI in 1457, and revised a few years later around 1463. That it was popular is indicated by the twelve manuscript copies which survive, by the fact that it was used by Malory, and that it was printed in 1543, becoming the base for Grafton's *Chronicles*.[41] Hardyng's work is derived from the usual sources, including Nennius, Bede, Geoffrey, Henry of Huntingdon and Ranulph Higden: and in conflating them he, like Higden, makes Severus' Wall run 'From Tynmouth to Alclud'.[42]

What makes Hardyng particularly interesting from the perspective of this work, however, is that he came from Northumberland, and was at one time constable of Warkworth Castle in that county. It is not unreasonable to suppose he could have seen the southern wall, and this supposition is strengthened, first, by the fact that, nearly a hundred years before Leland, he called it by what seems to have been the local name, namely 'the pyghte wall' (The Picts' Wall). Although, as will be shown later, that name goes back at least to the thirteenth century, Hardyng seems to be the first chronicler to have used it: indeed, it is possible that Leland may merely have borrowed that name from Hardyng, as Hearne's *Collectanea* includes a copy of a Leland note taken from Hardyng to the effect that 'sum say that Alcluith ... stoode at the end of the Picthe walle'.[43]

Secondly, although still in part paraphrasing Bede, Hardyng

[39] Babington, **I**, x & **II**, 72.
[40] J. Taylor, *The Universal Chronicle of Ranulph Higden* (Oxford, 1966). See especially ch. viii, 135-148.
[41] H. Summerson, 'Hardyng John, b. 1377/8, d. in or after 1464', *Oxford Dictionary of National Biography*, 2004, **25**, 240-243.
[42] R. Grafton, *The Chronicle of Jhon* (sic) *Hardyng* (London, 1543) (Early English Books On-Line), fol. xiv. H. Ellis (ed.), *The Chronicle of John Hardyng* (London, 1812).
[43] T. Hearne, *Joannis Lelandi Antiquarii de Rebus Britannicis Collectanea* (London, 1770), **III**, 425.

seems also to have given a possible eye-witness account which includes the first-ever mention of the milecastles, more than a hundred years before Christopher Ridley:

Thys legyon and Brytons hole assembled
That made a wal wel wrought of lyme and stone
Where Sever made of turves and soddes sembled
With castels strong and toures for the nones
At eche myles ende to agaynstand al the foonyse
From sea to sea as yet it is wel sene
In divers places, where it was wont to bene.[44]

The new approach of the humanists

Although Hardyng added his own observations, his work as a whole was still very much a re-hashing of the old sources. However, 'new' classical sources were starting to become available in print, such as Caesar (1469), Pliny (1469), Tacitus (1470), and, most importantly of all from the perspective of this paper, the *Scriptores Historiae Augustae,* which contained an account of Hadrian, attributed to one Aelius Spartianus.[45] This work was known from a ninth century copy, and had circulated in manuscript – but the first printed edition (Milan, 1475) had made it available for the first time to a wider audience, while the Aldine editions of 1516 and 1519, and Erasmus' edition of 1518, printed at Basel, spread its fame still further.[46] Today, the six authors of the *Scriptores* are all assumed to be one man, and the general conclusion is that the most likely culprit is Ammianus Marcellinus, who wrote the whole work, much of the later parts of which are now known to be largely fictional, about the year 395.[47] However early-modern historians had no reason to doubt that it was an authentic history, dating perhaps

---

[44] Hardyng, fol. liii. '*foonyse*', which rhymes with 'stone' and 'nones', appears to be a plural of 'foe'.

[45] For dates of first printed editions, see D. Hay, (ed. & trans.), *The Anglica Historia of Polydore Vergil A.D. 1485-1537,* Camden 3rd Series, **LXXIV**, 1950, xviii.

[46] The full text in Latin and English is available in D. Magie (trans.), *The Scriptores Historiae Augustae,* **I**, (London, 1922). A more recent translation of the first part, including the lives of Hadrian and Severus, is in A. Birley, *Lives of the Later Caesars* (Harmondsworth, 1976), cap. xi, 68.

[47] R. Syme, *Ammianus and the Historia Augusta* (Oxford, 1968). See especially ch. xiv, 72-79 & ch. xxx, 220.

from the reign of Constantine, and written by Spartianus and five other authors. For the purposes of this paper, the *Augustan History* will be viewed through those early-modern eyes. The significance of Spartianus is that he was the sole classical source to state that Hadrian was the first to build a wall in Britain. He used the word *murus*, not *vallum*, and said it was 80 miles long, built to separate barbarians and Romans.[48] Also in the *Augustan History*, there is an account of Antoninus Pius, attributed to Julius Capitolinus, which records the building by Lollius Urbicus of a second wall, this one of turf (*murus cespiticius*): while the *Augustan History* of Severus, again attributed to Spartianus, mentions that the glory of that emperor's reign was the wall he built across the island.[49]

The first to incorporate this new information into a chronicle, though without naming it as his source, seems to have been the Scot, Hector Boece (or Boyce, also known as Boethius). Boece, from Dundee, studied in Paris in the 1480s, where he became friendly with Erasmus (who edited an edition of the *Augustan History* in 1518). A proponent of humanist learning, Boece returned to Scotland and in 1505 became the first principal of the new university of King's College, Aberdeen.[50] His great work, the *Scotorum Historia* was published in Latin in 1527, and translated into Scots, at the time a very distinctive variety of English, by John Bellenden (or Ballantyne).[51] In this account, Boece set out to place the Scots at the centre of the history of this island and, amongst other things, to disprove the English contention that the Picts were relative newcomers:

---

[48] Magie, I, 'Hadrian', cap. xi, 34-5. Birley, *Lives*, 68. The key texts are also quoted in the original Latin in Hodgkin, *Literary History*, 106. It is worth noting that an even earlier attribution to Hadrian may be the recently discovered Staffordshire Moorlands Pan, which is similar in many ways to the Rudge cup and Amiens *patera* (see note 105 below). In listing places along the Wall, this *may* show that the Wall was known in the second century as the Wall of Aelius (= Hadrian). Part of the inscription reads ... RIGOREVALIAELIDRACONIS ..., which could be read *either* as 'on the line of the Aelian Wall, [the property] of Draco': *or* as 'on the line of the Wall, [the property] of Aelius Draco'. See *Britannia*, 35, 2004, 326, 344-5.

[49] Magie, I, 'Antoninus', cap. v, 110-111, 'Severus', cap. xviii, 412-3: Birley, *Lives*, 100, 218.

[50] N. Royan, 'Hector Boece (*c*.1465-1536)', *Oxford Dictionary of National Biography*, 2004, 6, 418-421.

[51] For a description of some of the varieties of English at this date, see C. Barber, *Early Modern English* (Edinburgh, 1976).

11

this Ile of Albioun wes inhabit fra the beginning thairof with thre sindry pepill, that is to say, Britonis, Scottis, and Pichtis.[52]

Utilising the newly available classical sources, Boece incorporated Tacitus into his chronicle, again apparently the first to do so, naming him as his source for his accounts of Claudius, Vespasian, *Caratak, Cartumanda, Uodicta quene of the Britons*, of Julius Frontinus, of Julius Agricola's campaigns beyond *the wod of calidon*, and much more. It is, however, his report of Hadrian's reign which is most important in terms of the present work, and it is worth quoting at some length from Bellenden's translation of *the fyft Buke, Ca iiii*, (1536 edn.), entitled 'How Adriane emprioure come in Britane, and biggit an strang wall ...'[53]

Adriane ... beildit ane huge wall of fail and deuait[54] rycht braid and hie in maner of ane hill fra the mouth of Tyne fornens[55] the Almaine seis to the flude of Esk fornens the Ireland seis. This was was lxxx mylis of length. It is said in our croniklis that this dike wes begun be Adriane and endit be Seuerus the Romane empriour. And callit the wal of Seueir. Bot we followyng Ueremond callis it the wal of Adriane fra the first foundoure.

If Boece is right that there were earlier chronicles which attributed the building of the wall to Hadrian, then they are lost. Although his story seems to come directly from Spartianus, Boece himself gives one Veremond as his authority for calling it Hadrian's Wall. Unfortunately, no-one apart from Boece has before or since ever heard of Veremond: and, as Royan in the *Dictionary of National Biography* entry says, 'it is common to question whether such material ever existed independently of Boece'.[56]

---

[52] H. Boece, *Heir beginnis the hystory and croniklis of Scotland*, 1540 (Early English Books On-Line). The quote is John Bellenden's Scots translation, the opening 'Cosmographe and discription', Ch. iii. See also R. W. Chambers et al, *The Chronicles of Scotland, compiled by Hector Boece, Translated from the Scots by John Bellenden, 1531*, Scottish Text Society, 3rd Series, 10 & 15, 1938-41.

[53] Boece, *Croniklis*, 5th book, Ch. iiii. 'biggit' = built.

[54] 'fail and deuait' = fail and divot (= turf and sod). M. Robinson (ed.), *The Concise Scots Dictionary* (Aberdeen, 1985) gives 'fail' as 'turf as a material for building or roofing' (185) and 'divot' as 'a piece of turf thinner than a fail' (151).

[55] 'fornens' = facing, alongside.

[56] Royan, *Boece*, DNB.

Leaving aside the question of Boece's sources, the important thing is that, despite mentioning elsewhere that it was repaired under Severus, over and over again Boece calls the southern wall 'the wal of Adriane', thus distinguishing it from the northern wall built in the time of Theodosius, when

Uictorine capitane of Britane commandit the Britonis be general edict to byg ye wal betuix Abircorne and Dunbritane with staik and ryse in thair strangest maner.[57]

Boece calls this northern wall either 'the wal of Abircorn', or 'Grahamis dike' after Graham, who, just before the appeal to Aetius (which Gildas had mentioned, dating it by implication to the mid-fifth century)

brak doun the same in all partis so halelie, that he left na thyng thairof standyng more than remainis nowe in thir dayis.[58]

However, whilst these words could possibly imply that Boece had personally visited the northern wall, he made no similar remark about Hadrian's Wall, merely saying it was 'bet doun to ye ground' at the same time.

The next humanist scholar to address the question of the Wall appears to have followed in Boece's footsteps, at least in terms of its attribution. This was Polydore Vergil, who used Boece as one of many sources for his *Historia Anglica*, published in 1534.[59] Vergil, a friend of Erasmus, Thomas More and other renaissance scholars, adopted a critical approach to the study of history, an approach which led him to reject the Brutus myth and, like Boece before him, to reject the more extravagant stories of Arthur. An Italian, he came to England in 1502, and had completed a manuscript history of his adopted country by 1513, although he continued to revise it prior to its publication in Basel in 1534, with further revised editions in 1546 and 1556.[60] An anonymous manuscript translation of it exists

---

[57] Boece in fact says it was 'Anthonius' (that is, Caracalla) who repaired the wall, 5th book, ca. xv. The 'wal betuix Abircorne' quote is from Boece, 7th book, chapter ii. 'Byg' = build. 'Ryse' here is probably used in the sense of bank or rampart. 'Strangest' = strongest.

[58] Boece, 7th book, chapter xvi. 'Halelie' = wholly, completely.

[59] Polydori Vergilii Vrbinatis *Anglicae Historiae Libri Vigintiseptem* (Basel, 1556).

[60] W. J. Connell, 'Polydore Vergil, *c.*1470-1555', *Oxford Dictionary of National Biography*, 2004, **56**, 323-327. See also the Introduction in D. Hay (ed. & trans.), *The Anglica Historia of Polydore Vergil A.D. 1485-1537*, Camden 3rd Series, **LXXIV**, 1950.

in the British Library, written in 'hands of the third quarter of the XVI century': however Vergil's work never seems to have been very popular in England, and the contemporary translation, quotations from which are used below, was not printed until 1846.[61]

Vergil used all the latest available classical authors, as had Boece: and he also used Gildas (a critical edition of whose work Polydore Vergil himself had brought out in 1525), Bede, William of Malmesbury and Matthew Paris (copies of works of both these authors with Vergil's marginal notes exist in the British Library), Henry of Huntingdon, Ranulph Higden and many others.[62] In his account of the Wall, having referred to Spartianus as his source, although adding details from Boece (such as its terminus at the Esk), he was unequivocal about its founder. Although he noted that some authorities attributed it to Severus, 'wee declare that Hadrianus didde bylde it: thus the doctors dissente'.[63]

Vergil went on to say that, although some say the wall was 'of sownde and whole stone, the trackes wherof are at this day permanent', Gildas said it was originally built of turf, but that the wall was later rebuilt with stone 'which at this time, although not wholie, maye bee perceived bie the littel embattled towers in aequall space distant'.[64] Although it is possible that this is another paraphrase of or gloss on Bede, it could also be interpreted as a first-hand eyewitness account by Vergil of the Wall, and its milecastles.[65]

It is certainly not impossible that Vergil could have seen the southern wall. From 1502 to 1508, and again from 1512 to 1515, he was sub-collector of Peter's Pence, in which capacity he may well have travelled from diocese to diocese, perhaps visiting Carlisle and/or Durham on official business. However, Vergil seems com-

---

[61] British Library Royal MS 18 C. VIII, IX: H. Ellis (ed.), *Polydore Vergil's English History, from an early translation preserved among the manuscripts of the old Royal Library in the British Museum*, Camden Society, **36**, 1846 (Facsimile edition, Felinfach, 1996).

[62] British Library Royal MS 13 D. V (7) William of Malmesbury: Royal MS 14 C. VII Matthew Paris *Historia Anglorum*.

[63] Ellis, *Polydore Vergil's English History*: the Esk reference is on p. 84, the Hadrian reference on p. 87.

[64] Ellis, 87.

[65] Because of the significance of these quotations, it is perhaps important to give Vergil's own words, showing that the anonymous translator had not embellished what Vergil actually wrote. In the first reference Vergil said *cuius vestigia ad hanc quoque aetatem nostram extant* ('the remains of which exist still to this our age'): while the second reads *qui etiam nunc, etsi non integer, turribus aequis spatiis interpositis munitus uisitur* ('which yet now, although not entirely, is seen by the fortified towers, inserted at equal intervals'), Vergil, 1556 edn., Book 2, 44.

pletely unaware of the northern wall, despite his knowledge that Lollius Urbicus had served in the province under Antoninus: and so Vergil, as others had done before him, conflated the various accounts to come up with a composite version, whereby Hadrian built the original Wall, which was then later 'reaedified' not in the time of Severus, but 200 years later.[66]

And thus at this season was this wall made bie the captains sent of Aetius, not of Emperours Hadrianus or Severus, as manie menne have lefte in memorie verie falselie, if wee believe Gildas, a Brittyshe historiographer.[67]

The reaction of the nationalists

The fundamental problem with Boece and Vergil, in terms of acceptance of their accounts, was that they were respectively Scots and Italian. Boece was largely ignored by English writers, while Vergil was seen as being un-English or even anti-English, and was associated with papistry, which was a bit unfair, as Vergil had signed the 1536 articles. The venom which his views attracted has been described by Connell, who quoted the protestant historian John Bale as accusing Vergil of 'polutynge oure Enlgyshe chronycles most shamefullye with his Romishe lyes and other Italyshe beggerye'.[68] John Leland was equally incensed, in particular by Vergil's denial of the historicity of Arthur, and he wrote a book attacking Vergil's views, as well as an essay *contra Polydorum Vergilium*.[69] Meanwhile, Boece's self-satisfied, but somewhat exaggerated, claim that he took a rigidly critical view of his sources, was similarly hardly likely to endear him to Leland, or to any other English reader, particularly when Boece put Arthur on a par with Finn MacCool, the Irish Giant, concerning whom Boece had written:

Of quhome ar mony vulgar fabyllis amang ws nocht vnlyke to thir fabyllis that ar rehersit of kyng Arthure. And becaus his

---

[66] Ellis, 87.
[67] Ellis, 103.
[68] Connell, DNB.
[69] Both are reproduced in T. Hearne, *Joannis Lelandi Antiquarii de Rebus Britannicis Collectanea* **V**, (London, 1770), 2-68. If Bale is to be believed, the animosity was reciprocal: Bale describes Vergil as Leland's enemy. J. Bale, *The Laboryouse Journey & serche of Johan Leylande* (London, 1549) (Early English Books On-Line), unpaginated, Preface, fol. Biiii.

dedis is nocht authorist be authentik authouris. I wyll rehers na thing thairof.[70]

Leland, discussing Boece, said that the Scots' hatred of the Britons was proverbial, whilst in his *Encomia Illustrium Virorum* (published posthumously in 1589) Leland's comment on Boece was *quot mendacia scripsit* (what lies he wrote).[71] All of this seems to have ensured that the incorporation into the national story of the 'new' classic authorities favoured by Vergil and Boece, such as Tacitus and Spartianus, was somewhat delayed.

This seems to have been particularly the case with Leland, who was clearly familiar with Gildas, Bede and Nennius' accounts of the Wall(s), as can be seen from Hearne's *Collectanea* in which were reproduced notes, including all the relevant references from those three authors.[72] The *Collectanea* also includes extensive general notes taken from the later chroniclers, but the only one of these from whom Leland noted down any Wall references was Hardyng.[73] Moreover, Leland does not appear to have made any mention of Spartianus anywhere in his notes: and although he included *Cornelius Tacitus* in his list of sources for his *Assertio Inclytissimi Arturii Regis Britanniae*, and in his *Newe Yeares Gyfte* of 1546, he does not show any obvious signs of having read him.[74]

Given possible earlier visits by Higden, Hardyng and Vergil, Leland can no longer claim the title the first 'modern' eyewitness to the Wall: yet there is little doubt that he was the first to visit it and describe it in any detail, listing places along the route of the Wall from Bowness to Thirlwall, and recording 'betwyxt Thyrwal and North Tine', not just a good description of the Wall and its ditch, but also a description of the feature now called the Vallum:

Beside the stone wall, ther appere yet in very many places *vestigia muri cespititii,* that was an arow shot a this side the stone

---

[70] Boece, 7th book, Ch. xviii 'Of whom are many vulgar fables among us, not unlike the fables that are told of King Arthur. And because his [i.e. Finn MacCool's] deeds are not authenticated by authoritative authors, I will not repeat anything of them'.

[71] Hearne, **V**, 40, 126.

[72] Hearne, **III**, 46, 48, 66, 124, 125, 160.

[73] Hearne, **III**, 425.

[74] Hearne, **V**, 16: Toulmin Smith, **I**, xli: Leland's 'New Years' Gift' was also published, with a commentary, in J. Bale, *The Laboryouse Journey & serche of Johan Leylande* (London, 1549) (Early English Books On-Line).

ILLUSTRATIONS

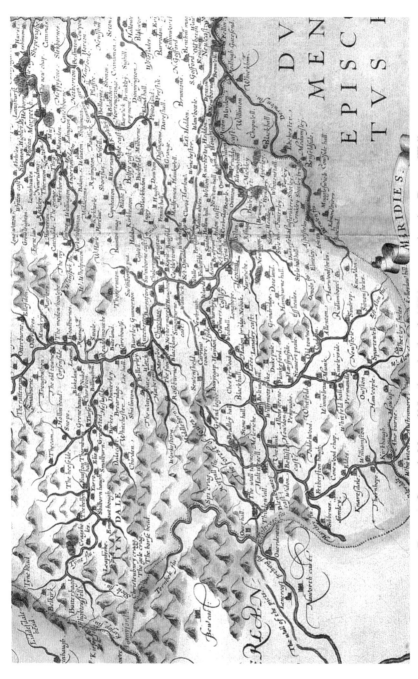

PLATE 1. Saxton's Map of Northumberland, 1576: extract showing Roman Wall.
British Library, Royal Ms.18.D.III. fol. 71v-72. Reproduced by permission of the British Library.

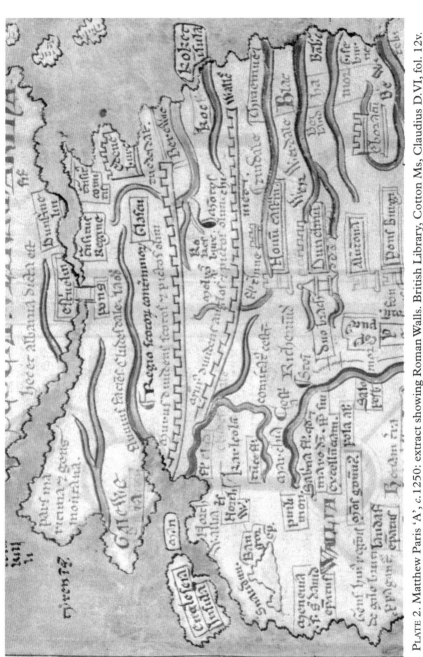

PLATE 2. Matthew Paris 'A', *c.* 1250: extract showing Roman Walls. British Library, Cotton Ms, Claudius D.VI, fol. 12v. Reproduced by permission of the British Library.

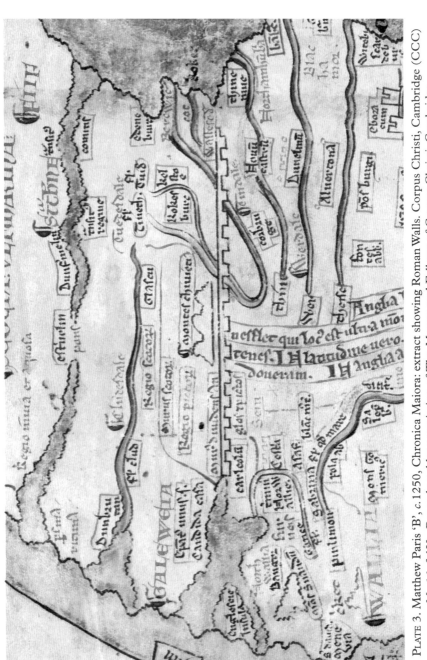

PLATE 3. Matthew Paris 'B', c.1250, Chronica Maiora: extract showing Roman Walls. Corpus Christi, Cambridge (CCC) Ms 16, folVv. Reproduced by permission of The Master and Fellows of Corpus Christi, Cambridge.

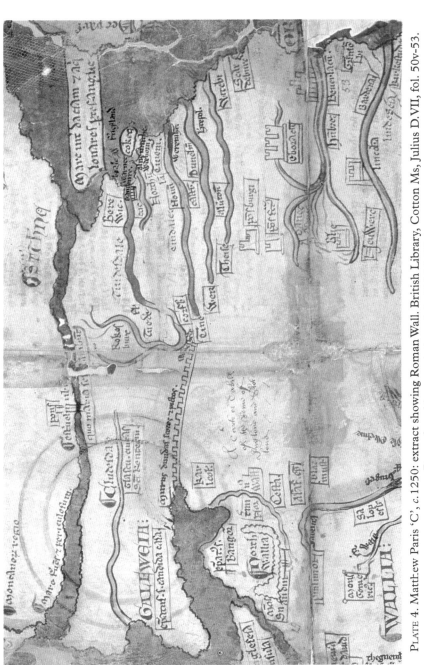

PLATE 4. Matthew Paris 'C', c. 1250: extract showing Roman Wall. British Library, Cotton Ms, Julius D.VII, fol. 50v-53. Reproduced by permission of the British Library.

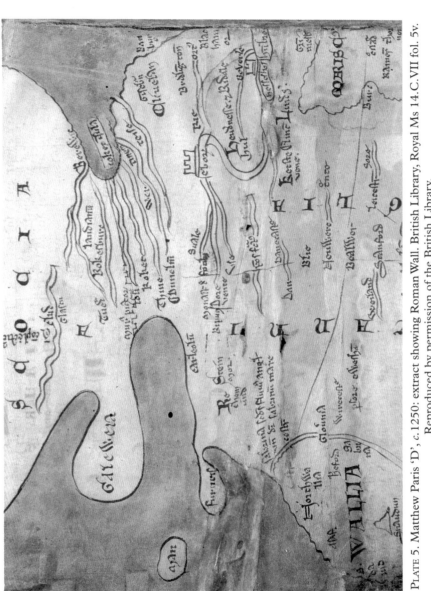

PLATE 5. Matthew Paris 'D', c.1250: extract showing Roman Wall. British Library, Royal Ms 14.C.VII fol. 5v. Reproduced by permission of the British Library.

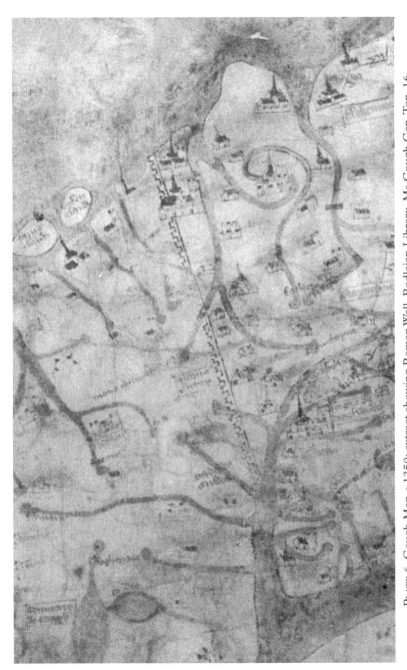

PLATE 6. Gough Map c. 1350: extract showing Roman Wall. Bodleian Library, Ms Gough Gen. Top. 16. Reproduced by permission of the Bodleian Library, University of Oxford.

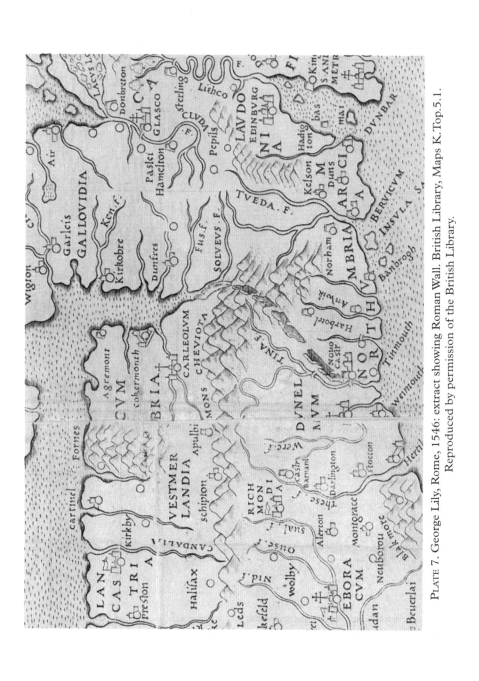

PLATE 7. George Lily, Rome, 1546: extract showing Roman Wall. British Library, Maps K.Top.5.1. Reproduced by permission of the British Library.

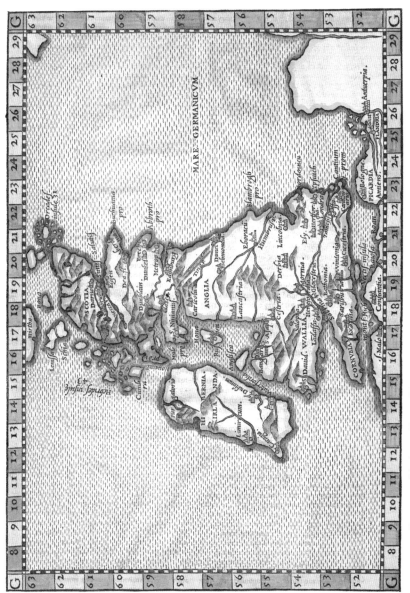

PLATE 8. Giralomo Ruscelli, Venice, 1561. This edition Paris, 1575. (Private Collection).

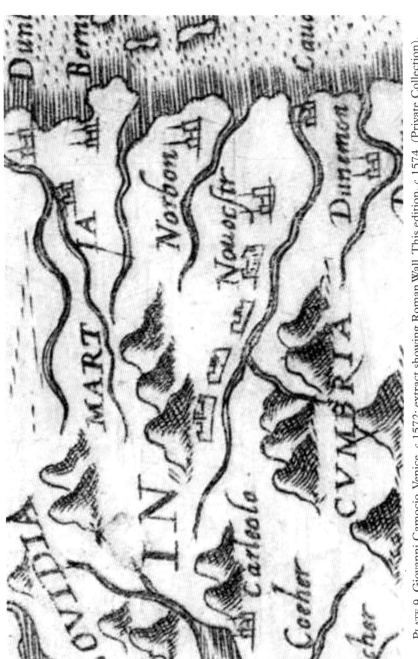

PLATE 9. Giovanni Camocio, Venice, c.1572: extract showing Roman Wall. This edition, c.1574. (Private Collection).

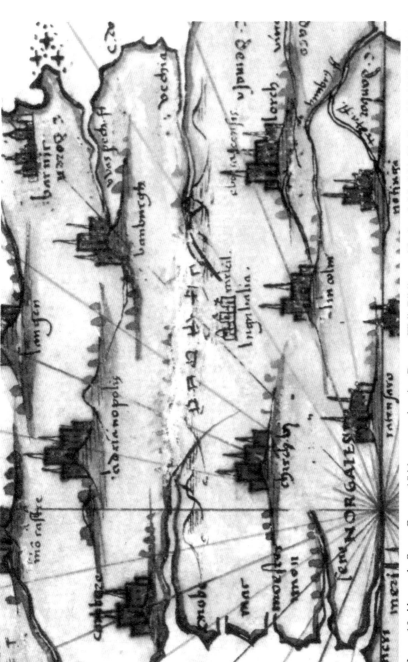

PLATE 10. Alonso de Santa Cruz, *c*.1546: extract showing Roman Wall. Biblioteca Nacional, Madrid, Ms Res. 38, 1545, fol. 60v. Reproduced by permission of the Biblioteca Nacional de España.

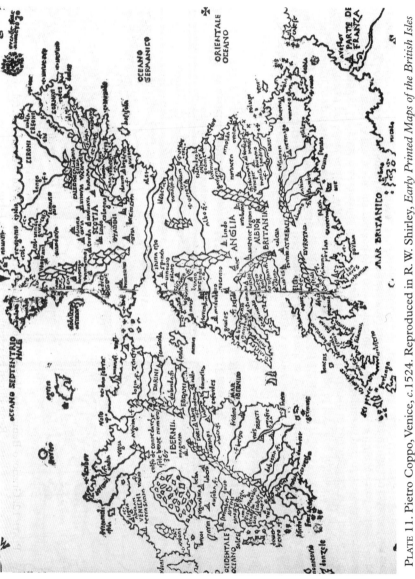

PLATE 11. Pietro Coppo, Venice, c.1524. Reproduced in R. W. Shirley, *Early Printed Maps of the British Isles 1477-1650*, Revised edn, 1991.

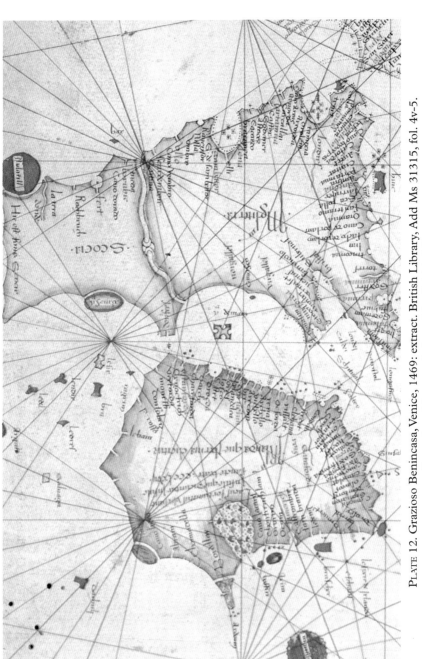

PLATE 12. Grazioso Benincasa, Venice, 1469: extract. British Library, Add Ms 31315, fol. 4v-5. Reproduced by permission of the British Library.

PLATE 13. Martin Waldseemüller, Strasbourg, 1513: extract showing Solway-Tyne line. (Private Collection).

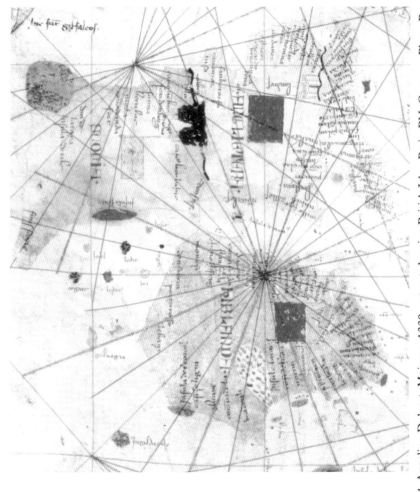

PLATE 14. Angelino Dulcert, Majorca, 1339: extract showing British Isles. Paris, BN, Cartes et Plans, Res. Ge B 696. Reproduced by permission of Bibliothèque Nationale de France. The image is here inverted: the original has south at the top.

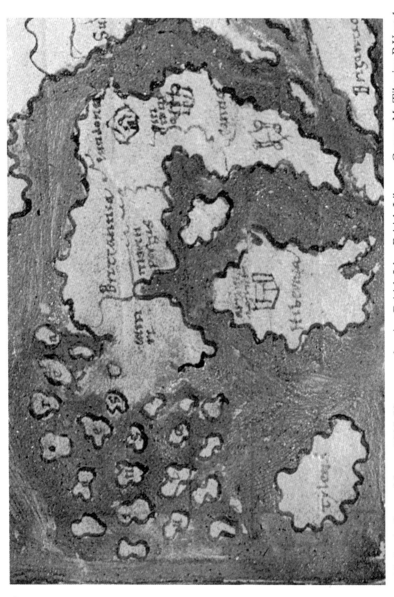

PLATE 15. Anglo-Saxon Map, c.1025–50: extract showing British Isles. British Library, Cotton Ms Tiberius B.V. pt 1, fol. 56v. Reproduced by permission of the British Library. The map of the whole known world measures 21 cm x 17 cm. The above extract measures only c.5cm x 4 cm on the original, and is here reproduced about three times life size.

wal: but that it was thoroughly made as the stone wal was yt doth not wel appeare there.[75]

Although the descriptions in his *Itinerary* are well known, yet Leland's equally important, though possibly second-hand, observations in Hearne's *Collectanea* seem to have been largely ignored. In Vol. IV, under the interesting 'catch-all' heading of *Murus Picticus, Vallum praetorianum, Vallum Hadrianicum, Vallum Severianum*, Leland noted that there were visible remains of the Wall at Walker near Wallsend, and also at Denton, where they are *nec humiles nec infirmi*.[76] He went on to report that one Doctor Hyliard, the cousin of Doctor Robert Ridley (a theologian who died *c.*1536) lived in a tower on the Wall, and that 'Ruge Dragon' had asserted that there were a number of castles or towers built from the remains of the Wall. Leland conjectured from this that not long before his time a much greater part of the Wall must have been intact, before it was demolished for use in neighbouring buildings (a point he also made, but more briefly, in his *Itinerary*).[77]

Leland's reference to *Vallum Praetorianum* would appear to derive from the Antonine Itinerary, a copy of which had appeared in print by 1518.[78] In the *Iter Britaniarvm* (sic), the first route is headed *A limite id est a vallo praetorio usque MP CLVI*.[79] This would appear to mean 'from the border, that is, from the rampart all the way to *Praetorium* (probably a garbled version of *Petuaria* = Brough on Humber), 156 miles': however, Leland seems to have read this as 'from the border, that is from the headquarters rampart, all the way, 156 miles'.[80]

---

[75] 'the remains of a wall of turf': Toulmin Smith, 5, 60-61.

[76] Hearne, **IV**, 42. 'Neither stunted nor feeble' (i.e. upstanding and substantial).

[77] *Ruge dragon asseruit, castella aliquot & turres vel hoc nostro seculo ex valli reliquiis reparata fuisse. Unde probabilis conjectura, ante aliquod secula magnam muri partem integram fuisse, donec in usus aedificiorum demoliebatur.* Hearne, *Collectanea*, **IV**, 42. For Robert Ridley, see R. Rex, 'Robert Ridley, d.1536?', *Oxford Dictionary of National Biography*, 2004, **46**, 954-955. Which tower house is meant here is not clear, but the Ridley family were located at Ridley Hall which stood on the banks of the South Tyne, near Haydon Bridge.

[78] *Itinerarivm Antonini Avg* (included in a collection with Pomponius Mela, Julius Solinus and other writers, Venice, in aedibus Aldi et Andreae Soceri, 1518). The second route also starts *a vallo*.

[79] *Itinerarivm*, 1518, fol. 178. For the identification of *Praetorium*, see A. L. F. Rivet & C. Smith, *The Place Names of Roman Britain* (London, 1981), 155, 437.

[80] The first detailed commentary on the *Itinerary*, having suggested, following Camden, that the *id est a vallo* may be a later insertion, translates it as 'From the *Limes*, or bounds, to *Praetorium*', W. Burton, *A Commentary on Antoninus, his Itinerary* (London, 1658), 34-36.

Leland, in the alternative names quoted in his catch-all heading, apparently admitted of the possibility that there might have been a *vallum Hadrianicum:* yet it remains likely that he would probably have argued strongly the over-riding case for Bede's 'mural theory', namely that the Vallum was constructed under Severus, while the stone Wall was built in the early-fifth century. Indeed, during the first three-quarters of the sixteenth century, chroniclers and printers generally, despite the new 'mural theories' of Boece and Vergil, continued to reproduce for the general reader this accepted version of the story. Thus Robert Fabyan's *Chronicle*, first published 1516, and republished in 1533, 1542 and 1559, and sometimes regarded as the first chronicle of the modern era, was heavily based on Ranulph Higden, and had nothing to say on the Wall that did not come from that source.[81] Rastell's *Pastyme of People* (1530) similarly repeats the standard account, while Richard Grafton, catering for the growing popular market for such works, produced first his edition of Hardyng, then his own *Abridgement of the Chronicles of England* (1562) and then a more substantial *Chronicle at Large* (1568), all of which start with the *Brut*, and, so far as the Wall is concerned, merely repeat the familiar Severan and fifth century stories.[82]

There was, however, one scholar who, whilst as anti-Boece and anti-Vergil as had been Leland, was nevertheless prepared to take an open-minded look at the new evidence. This was Humfrey Lhuyd of Denbigh (1527-1568), an antiquarian and map-maker who had built up an impressive library which later became the basis for the Royal Collection in the British Library.[83] Lhuyd had met Abraham Ortelius in Antwerp around 1566, and had sent him a map of England and Wales which Ortelius subsequently published in his hugely popular and influential *Theatrum Orbis Terrarum* of 1573. Lhuyd had also sent to Ortelius an accompanying account of Britain, in Latin, which was subsequently 'Englished' by one Thomas Twyne, and published in 1573 as *The Breuiary of Britayne*.[84] In the *Breviary*, Lhuyd explained how he had 'chaunced

---

[81] R. Fabyan, *The Chronicle of Fabyan* (London, 1542) (Early English Books On-Line), 44, 57.

[82] J. Rastell, *The Pastyme of People* (London, 1530): unpaginated, fol.Ci. R. Grafton, *Abridgement of the Chronicles of England* (London, 1562), fol.14: R. Grafton, *Chronicle at Large* (London, 1569), 84. All via Early English Books On-Line.

[83] R. Brinley Jones, 'Humphrey Llwyd (1527-1568)', *Oxford Dictionary of National Biography*, 2004, **34**, 174-176.

[84] H. Lhuyd, *The Breuiary of Britayne* (London, 1573) (Early English Books On-Line).

of late yeres to come to the sight of Polydorus Virgilius the Italian, and Hector Boethius the Scot'. Although accusing the former of attempts to 'defame the Britaynes them selves with scandalous lies', and the latter of being 'a foolish writer', nevertheless Lhuyd said that, having read them:

I began to peruse all suche auncient hystories, both Greke and Latine, as ever had writen of Britayne or the Britaynes.[85]

On the basis of that research, which included reading Tacitus, Dion (= Cassius Dio), Herodian, Ammianus Marcellinus, Spartianus and Capitolinus, Lhuyd was able not only to demolish Boece's more extravagant claims concerning the Scots: but he also concluded that:

This limityng wall (as Spartianus reporteth) was first buildeth by Adrianus the Emperour, fourscore myles in length. And Capitolinus is author, that Antoninus erected another made of Turfes, between the Britaynes. And last of all, that Seuerus, by a trenche which was cast from Sea, to Sea: deuided the Roman prouince from the other Britains all men do generally agree. Whereby our countrymen call it *Mur Seuerus*, that is to say: Seuerus wall, and in another place *Gual Seuerus*, Seuerus vally, at this day.[86]

Elsewhere in the *Breviary*, in a reference to the Antonine Itinerary, Lhuyd picked up the term previously noted from Leland, namely the 'Vally Praetorius', adding:

for that there was a vally from the river *Soluathianus* to the mouth of Tine: al do knowe.[87]

Twyne's translation of Lhuyd's *vallum* (= British *gual*) as 'vally' is most odd, and is clearly related to the use of the word 'trenche' in the previous quotation: while Camden similarly, though later, noted Æthelweard's emphasis on Severus' *fossa*, which appeared in Philemon Holland's translation of Camden's *Britannia* as 'a ditch or

---

[85] Lhuyd, fol. 7.
[86] Lhuyd, fol. 48.
[87] Lhuyd, *Breuiary*, fol. 30.

trenche'.[88] Holland's translation also said that the Anglo-Saxon Chronicle had reported that 'Severus foregirdled and fenced Britain with a ditch from sea to sea': yet the Saxon word Camden had used here, *dic*, dyke, is at least as likely to mean embankment as ditch.[89]

Polydore Vergil had similarly confused the concepts, basing his account upon Herodian, and saying that Severus had set limits to the province, 'bileding a wall like a trenche.[90] Lhuyd too, and Camden subsequently, seem to have given weight to the reference in Herodian to what Camden in his first (Latin) edition merely calls χῶμα: but which appears in the English edition as 'χῶμα, that is, a Trench or Fosse cast up'.[91] Although Collingwood says Herodian is not here specifically referring to the Wall, and indeed the Greek word 'may refer to continuous fortifications, but need mean no more than camps or forts', nevertheless Lhuyd seems to have taken this reference in Herodian, together with Bede's (or Orosius') account of a *magna fossa* built across the island under Severus, to mean the wide and deep ditch, flanked by mounds on either side, which lies just to the south of the Wall, which was remarked upon by Leland, and which is still known today as the Vallum.[92]

There are possibly also here in Lhuyd echoes of an apparently widespread earlier belief, to be found depicted on maps derived from the portolan chart tradition, that Scotland was, or had been, separated from England by a channel from sea to sea along the Solway-Tyne line. This seems to have existed in parallel with the knowledge, which goes back at least to Tacitus' *Agricola*, that the more-northerly part of Britain was separated from the rest by a narrow isthmus between the Forth and Clyde.[93] This latter isthmus is in medieval maps sometimes so reduced until it merely comprises the bridge of Stirling: but the

---

[88] *Chronicorum Ethelwerdi Libri IIII* (London, 1596). See also Camden, 1637 edn., trans. P. Holland, 791.

[89] Camden, 1637 edn., 791. H. Sweet, *Student's Dictionary of Anglo-Saxon* (Oxford, 1911) gives 'wall of earth, embankment' as the prime meaning, but also gives 'ditch, moat' as alternatives.

[90] Ellis, *Vergil*, 87. The Latin reads *murumque instar ualli fecisse:* did the translator mistake *vallum -i* (n), a rampart for *valles -is* (f) a valley? or had the word *vallum* come to mean an entrenchment by this date?

[91] Camden, 1587 edn., 532: 1637 edn., 789.

[92] Collingwood, 42. Collingwood uses the form χώματα (Herodian, Book III, under A.D. 211). S. Ireland, *Roman Britain, A Sourcebook* (London, 1986) translates this passage as 'the rivers and earthworks on the frontier of the Roman Empire', 111.

[93] H. Mattingly (trans.: revised by S. A. Handford), *Tacitus: The Agricola and the Germania,* (Harmondsworth, 1970 edn.), ch. 23, 74.

two mapping traditions, which will be commented upon in more detail later, appear to be separate. Lhuyd as a map collector could well have been aware of maps in the portolan-chart style, showing the Solway-Tyne line as a channel, reinforcing his ideas of a Severan 'trenche' or 'vally' (see Plates 11 & 12).

With Lhuyd, the stage was set for Camden: but in the meantime, another chronicler, and another map-maker, had added considerably to contemporary detailed knowledge of the Wall, namely William Harrison and Christopher Saxton. In 1997, B. J. N. Edwards drew attention to the fact that William Harrison's account, in the first volume of Raphaell Holinshed's *Chronicles* (1577), had specified Hadrian as the 'author and beginner' of the Wall, quoting Spartianus; and had given a detailed listing of all the places through which the Wall passed, based in part upon Leland, but continuing east naming places not mentioned by Leland, from Walltown to Denton.[94] The source of this eastern information was settled in another article in 2001, when it was demonstrated that Harrison had used a manuscript or pre-publication draft of Christopher Saxton's *c.*1576 survey of Northumberland, without acknowledgement, to supply the missing place-names (Plate 1).[95]

The Wall in early maps

Saxton showed, and named, 'The Wall of the Pictes' on his maps of Northumberland, of Cumberland & Westmorland (1576), and on his 1583 wall-map of England.[96] He was the first to name most of the places along the Wall, and the first to attempt to chart it with any degree of geographical accuracy. He was not, however, by any means the first cartographer to depict the Wall on a map. Although long known and commented upon by cartographic historians at least as far back as Gough's *British Topography* (1780), historians of the Wall itself seem generally not to have noted or remarked upon this fact, with one recent exception, Alan Whitworth, who included illustrations of four pre-Camden maps showing the Wall in his

---

[94] B. J. N. Edwards, 'Raphaell Holinshed's description of Hadrian's Wall', *Hadrianic Society Bulletin*, January 1997, 7-8.

[95] B. J. N. Edwards & W. D. Shannon, 'Raphaell Holinshed's description of Hadrian's Wall', *CW3*, i, 2001, 196-201.

[96] W. Ravenhill, *Christopher Saxton's 16th Century maps: The Counties of England & Wales* (Shrewsbury, 1992): R. A. Skelton, *Saxton's Survey of England and Wales, with a facsimile of Saxton's wall-map of 1583* (Amsterdam, 1974).

account of the post-Roman influence of the Wall.[97] Whitworth also mentioned in his text several post-Camden maps showing the Wall, including William Hole's Anglo-Saxton Heptarchy map of 1607, produced for the sixth edition of Camden's *Britannia*. Noting that this map used 'a script which purports to be Anglo-Saxon', he was unable to explain why 'The Wall is marked as *Pelitter Peal*?'[98] In fact, however, this reads *Pehittes Weal*, that is, the Picts Wall.[99]

Gough's *British Topography*

In 1780 Richard Gough had published in his *Topography* engravings of four medieval maps which show the Wall, comprising three of the four versions of Matthew Paris' map of *c.*1250, while Gough's fourth illustration was the map which he had purchased in a manuscript sale of 1774, and which has ever since borne his name, the Gough map of *c.*1350.[100] Gough himself did not make much of the depiction of the Wall, merely noting its existence within his listing of all the place-names on these maps.[101] However, the fact that the oldest detailed maps of Britain which have come down to us all depict the Wall (or Walls), is of considerable significance, and is worth discussing in detail.

Matthew Paris' depictions of the Wall (Plates 2-5)

In addition to the three Gough plates, good quality colour reproductions of the full series of four maps produced by Matthew Paris around the year 1250 have been readily available to scholars

[97] R. Gough, *British Topography, or An Historical Account of what has been done for illustrating the Topographical Antiquities of Great Britain & Ireland* (London, 1780), I, plates ii, iii, iv, vi: A. M. Whitworth, *Hadrian's Wall: Some aspects of its Post-Roman Influence on the Landscape*, BAR British Series, **296**, 2000, figs. 55-58.

[98] Whitworth, 38.

[99] The map is itself a redrawing of a map by William Rogers from the 1600 edition of Camden. Whitworth refers to the reproduction on p.212 in C. Moreland & D. Bannister, *Antique Maps* (London, 1993). Another reproduction can be found in R. W. Shirley, *Early Printed Maps of the British Isles 1477-1650* (East Grinstead, 1980), plate 99, 114. The Rogers map is plate 86, 95.

[100] Gough, *British Topography*, 1780. Three of the Matthew Paris maps are now in the British Library, **A** (Cotton MS, Claudius D.VI, fol. 12v), **C** (Cotton MS, Julius D VII, fol. 50v-53), **D** (Royal MS 14 C. VII fol. 5v). The fourth, **B**, is in Cambridge, Corpus Christi MS 16, fol. Vv). The Gough map is in the Bodleian, MS Gough Gen Top 16.

[101] Gough, *British Topography*, **I**, 63, 64, 70, 80.

since Gilson's edition of 1928.[102] The maps are conventionally known as A, B, C and D, although the order of production is not known: indeed Harvey suggests the reverse order, D first, then C, B and finally A.[103] This seems unlikely to the present writer, as the greater detail given to northern places on D compared with the others seems to place it later: however, it may not be possible to say more than Mitchell did, namely that D really belongs to a different series.[104]

Map A shows two stylised crenellated walls, the southernmost of which is described as *murus dividens anglos et pictos olim*: while that to the north is marked *murus dividens scotos et pictos olim*.[105] These terms show that Matthew Paris probably had Bede's account in mind, although he was reinterpreting it, and was certainly not misled by those of his fellow chroniclers who sought to make one wall of two. Map B also shows two walls, the southern marked *murus dividens anglos et pictos*, while the northern, shown merely by a single drawn line, is *murus scotorum*.[106] Map C just has one wall, running from Tyne to Solway.[107] Matthew did not name it: but a later hand, believed to be that of his friend and successor John of Wallingford, wrongly identified this as the Antonine Wall and wrote by it *murus dividens scotos et pictos*.[108]

Finally, Map D also has just one Wall, in roughly the same position as on C, but here called *murus pictorum*.[109] Whether Paris invented the name Picts' Wall, or whether is was by then already generally, or locally, in use cannot be known: but this seems to be

---

[102] J. P. Gilson & H. Poole, *Four maps of Great Britain designed by Matthew Paris about A.D. 1250* (London, 1928). For a discussion, including a commentary on the depiction of the walls, see J. B. Mitchell, 'The Matthew Paris Maps', *The Geographical Journal*, **81**, No 1, Jan 1933, 27-34.

[103] P. D. A. Harvey, 'Matthew Paris's Maps of Britain', in P. R. Coss & S. D. Lloyd (eds.), *Thirteenth Century England*, **IV** (Woodbridge, 1991), 115.

[104] J. B. Mitchell, 'The Matthew Paris Maps', 27-34.

[105] British Library, Cotton MS, Claudius, D.VI, fol. 12v. It is worth noting that the only contemporary depictions of the Wall that we have, those on the Amiens *patera*, the very similar Rudge Cup and the Hildburgh fragment, all probably dating from some time in the second century, each shows a crenellated wall (see note 48, above).

[106] Corpus Christi, Cambridge, MS 16: Vv. Mitchell sees the northern wall here as a misinterpretation by Matthew Paris' copyist of an indistinct feature on an earlier map, which was actually the river Esk, 31.

[107] British Library, Cotton MS, Julius D.VII, fols. 50v–53r.

[108] Harvey, 'Matthew Paris's Maps of Britain', 116.

[109] British Library, Royal MS, 14c. VII, fol. 5v. See British Library catalogue for the reference to the Polydore Vergil notes.

the earliest surviving use of that title. It is worth noting, incidentally, that Polydore Vergil would definitely have seen this map, as the copy in the British Library of the *Historia Anglorum* with which it is bound bears notes in Vergil's handwriting.

Matthew Paris had became a monk at the Benedictine Abbey of St Albans in 1217, worked as a chronicler, and died there in 1259: but he was no recluse.[110] He is known to have accompanied the Court to Winchester and Westminster, and in 1248 was sent by the Pope to Norway. It is probable that he visited at one time or another various of the dependent priories and cells of St Albans Abbey, such as Belvoir, Tynemouth and Coquet Island (off the Northumbrian coast, near Alnwick), all of which feature on his maps. Indeed, the concept for his maps may have grown out of written itineraries describing places a day's journey apart on the route from St Albans to Tynemouth and beyond.[111] Based perhaps on his own experiences, but certainly also incorporating information he had received from monastic informants, the prime purpose of his maps, unusually for the period, seems to have been to help plan journeys. In that connection, the focus is on useful places, places through which a traveller might pass, or where he could spend the night. Rivers, as barriers to overland travel, are emphasised, but topographic or other features are otherwise ignored, with a few rare and specific exceptions. As the Walls are neither useful places, nor barriers to travel, it is difficult to explain why he decided to include them. There is a possibility, which will be explored later, that Matthew may have had an earlier source map which included one or more Walls: but even if he had had such a map, that does not explain his decision to incorporate that feature into his copy. However, an examination of the other exceptions to the 'utility' rule might throw some light on why these Walls were so depicted by Matthew.

Two mountain ranges are shown, Snowdon (on all four) and the Cheviots (on A & B only): yet these seem to be there less as barriers to movement than as something worthy of note, akin perhaps to the 'wonders of Britain', which feature in many of the chronicles going back to Nennius, but particularly to be found in Henry of Huntingdon, and those chronicles derived from him.[112] The only other natural feature on the Matthew Paris maps is *Pec*, on map A,

---

[110] R. Vaughan, *The Illustrated Chronicles of Matthew Paris* (Stroud, 1993), Introduction, vii-xiii.

[111] E. Edson, *Mapping Time and Space* (London, 1997), 118-125.

[112] Morris, *Nennius*, 40-3: Greenway, 22-23.

with the associated comment *eolus puteus ventorum* ('Aeolus cavern of the winds'). This was again a noted wonder, or even 'tourist attraction', first mentioned by Henry of Huntingdon, who reported on the winds 'which issues with such force from the caves in the mountain which is named the Peak'.[113] Other inscriptions on the Paris map refer to the people of Wales as descending from Brutus the Trojan. Taking this with the above features, it would appear to show not only familiarity on Paris' part with the 'native historians' and the chronicles, which is only to be expected: but more importantly, perhaps, it seems to imply a nationalist pride in the island of Britain, and in particular England, its history and its wonders.[114] It is probably in this light that Matthew's decision to include the Walls should be viewed, as still-impressive visible reminders of our heroic national past.

Unfortunately, although Matthew Paris set a new standard in practical mapping, his maps appear to have remained largely unknown outside his monastery of St Albans. He was ahead of his time, and his maps neither became general models, nor left direct successors: apart, that is, from the other medieval map to depict the Wall.[115]

The Wall on the Gough Map (Plate 6)

Gough's engraving of 1780 was superseded by the Ordnance Survey's reduced colour facsimiles of 1871 and 1935, and then by the OUP's facsimile and accompanying commentary of 1958.[116] Like Matthew Paris' maps, 'there is no doubt that its purpose was to serve as a map for travellers': moreover, the map appears to have been 'an official compilation for couriers or other servants of the Crown'.[117] It is all the more remarkable, then, that it depicts a crenellated feature, named *murus pictorum*, running in a straight line across the island from Tynemouth.

The way this feature is depicted is not unlike the Wall on Matthew

---

[113] Greenway, 22-23.

[114] Kathy Lavezzo has recently explored in depth the relationship between maps and ideas of nation in medieval England, although without mentioning either the Matthew Paris maps or the Gough map. K. Lavezzo, *Angels on the Edge of the World: Geography, Literature and English Community 1000-1534* (Ithaca, 2006).

[115] Harvey, 'Matthew Paris's Maps of Britain'.

[116] E. J. S. Parsons, *The Map of Great Britain c.A.D. 1360 known as the Gough Map: an introduction to the facsimile* (Oxford, 1958).

[117] Parsons, 15.

Paris B. In addition, the Gough map calls the Wall *murus pictorum*, as does Matthew Paris D: moreover Gough, like Matthew Paris B, shows both Snowdon and the Cheviots, and like Matthew Paris A, it names Peak Cavern (*Puteus Pek*). These parallels together imply that there must have been another Matthew Paris map, perhaps a definitive version, *E, which lies behind Gough. However, whether or not such an earlier map existed, the version of Gough which has come down to us dates from around 1350 or a little later. It is more accurate, and more detailed than Matthew Paris's thirteenth-century work by several orders of magnitude: and it shows signs of heavy use, the bottom edge being extremely worn, with the result that many names have been rubbed off, while others have been re-inked or overwritten.

How long the map that Gough discovered remained in use as a resource for official travellers, and how many subsequent copies and up-dates were made is impossible to say: but it was more than 200 years before anything better became available. It is certainly possible that Leland had seen a version of it, as he seems in Hearne's *Collectanea* to be describing a map of England which showed the Wall when he lists northern rivers taken *ex charta Topographica Angliae*. These are divided into three groups, the first comprising three *fluvii ultra murum in Tuedam devolvuntur*, followed by two rivers *trans murum*, then five rivers *citra murum inter Candidam casam et Wyrkinton in mare devolvuntur*.[118]

The Wall on the Lily map (Plate 7)

When the first maps of England came to be printed, it was perhaps no surprise that copies of the Gough map, at perhaps several stages removed from the version we have, should have been used. Thus Sebastian Munster had used either the Gough map or a derivative to produce woodcut maps of England in 1538 and 1540.[119] However, these did not include any representation of the Wall: whereas the first copper-plate map, indeed 'the first separately printed map of the whole of the British Isles', did so.[120] This was George Lily's map, printed in Rome in 1546.[121]

[118] Hearne, **IV**, 27: 'rivers beyond the wall flowing into Tweed': 'rivers across the wall': 'rivers this side of the wall, flowing into the sea between Whithorn and Workington'.
[119] Shirley, 15-16.
[120] Shirley, 22.
[121] E. Lynam, *The Map of the British Isles of 1546, with facsimile* (Jenkintown, 1934).

The cartographer Lily came from a world, and a home background, where the problem of the Wall could well have been discussed from time to time. He was the son of William Lily, a well-connected humanist scholar who had been John Leland's schoolmaster at St Paul's: and George was himself a friend of Polydore Vergil.[122] In 1529 he entered Reginald Pole's service, and moved with him to Rome in 1538, remaining then in Italy, and contributing four works to a major account of Britain, Paolo Giovio's *Descriptio Britanniae, Scotiae, Heperniae et Orchadum.* The copper-plate map may have been produced in connection with this.

Unlike Matthew Paris and the Gough map cartographer, both of whom had used a 'conventional' or symbolic representation of the Wall, Lily seems to have deliberately attempted something close to a realistic portrayal, showing it as a ruin, with both gateways and gaps: and not running straight across the island as the chroniclers had reported and as Gough had shown, but instead adopting a sinuous curve from Newcastle over the Cheviots to the Solway. It is difficult to resist the thought that, if Polydore Vergil had indeed seen the Wall himself, then he had subsequently described it to Lily.

Lily's map was enormously influential, and Shirley records twelve editions or directly derived versions between 1546 and 1602, while many other indirectly derived maps were also printed, many of which include the Wall, although in some versions it is all but unrecognisable. Thus that of Ruscelli, published in Venice in 1561 in an Italian language version of Ptolemy's *Geographia,* and republished in numerous other editions including a French language version of Munster's *Cosmographia,* in 1575, suggests that the engraver had no idea whatsoever as to what it was that he was supposed to be portraying. As a result, he shows the Wall as something like a ladder laid across the island (Plate 8).[123] On the other hand, Camocio's map of 1572, incorporated into one of the then-popular *Isole famose,* works describing the most famous islands of the world, shows a realistic view of the Wall, a re-interpretation rather than a mere copy of Lily (Plate 9).[124] What is clear from these

[122] The reference to 'Lily' being a friend of Vergil is from Hay, x/xi. Lynam, 2, makes it clear it is the son, not the father, who was Vergil's friend. R. D. Smith, 'William Lily 1468?-1522/*3*', *Oxford Dictionary of National Biography,* 2004, **33**, 801-803. T. F. Mayer, 'George Lily d.1559', Oxford *Dictionary of National Biography,* 2004, **33**, 799-800.

[123] Shirley, 34, 49, plates 36, 47.

[124] Shirley, 44, 47, plate 45.

examples is that, in the generation before Saxton and Camden, there were in circulation throughout Europe a significant number of copies of printed maps depicting the Wall, albeit some in a more recognisable form than others.

The manuscript map of Alonso de Santa Cruz (Plate 10)

This international awareness of the Wall can also be shown in the work of the Spanish cartographer Alonso de Santa Cruz who, more or less at the same time as Lily's map was first published, produced a manuscript map of Britain which included a portrayal of the Wall. A small, poor quality, monochrome reproduction of this map was published in 1918, with accompanying Spanish text.[125] Santa Cruz was from 1536 employed in Seville as *Cosmografo Real*, mainly on the *Padron General*, the top secret master map of the world, especially the New World.[126] In or about 1546, Santa Cruz produced a manuscript *Islario General de Todas Las Islas del Mundo*, as a gift for Don Phelipe, later Phillip II of Spain and husband of Mary Tudor. In his official capacity, all the latest maps would have been sent to Santa Cruz, and he is known to have had an extensive collection of maps, both manuscript and printed. He was also a historian, and his text on Britain in the *Isolario* attempted to reconcile the classical account of Britain found in Ptolemy with modern sources such as Polydore Vergil; and to place the resulting composite account onto a map which was derived from the Mediterranean *portolano* tradition rather than from Gough.

In his account of the Wall, Santa Cruz seems to have used both Vergil and another source, so far unidentified, which has turned Severus' 'trench' into a veritable canal across the island.[127]

Emperor Severus ... joined the river *Tueda* which came out of the eastern part of the said hills to the sea with another born in the same hills and heading west, taking the opportunity to

[125] The manuscript is undated and different sources give dates from 1540 to as late as 1560. However, it must date before Philip became king in 1556, while it almost certainly dates from after 1543 when Philip became Regent. The most likely date would appear to be *c*.1546. The text was published (in Spanish, with accompanying black & white maps) in D. A. Blasquez (ed.), *Islario General de Todas Las Islas del Mundo [1542]* (Madrid, 1918). The section on "Inglaterra" is at, **I**, 79-104.

[126] E. W. Dahlgren, *Map of the World by Alonso de Santa Cruz* (Stockholm, 1892).

[127] The translation below was commissioned by the author from Peter James of the University of Central Lancashire.

28

combine the two and make of them one which ran from sea to sea, joining the two seas which, with the passage of time, has broadened out and is shallow, because in summer you could wade across and in winter ships sail on it intent on plundering what they can. To this inlet of the sea the emperor Severus added a palisade or wall to the *Inglaterra* side so that the barbarians who had settled in *Scocia* should not pass, of which today only the remains and the memory thereof can be seen.[128]

The idea that England was divided from Scotland by a single channel, or two broad rivers with a common source, making Scotland almost, or completely, into an island, is a feature of the medieval marine charts known as portolans, and on maps derived from these, such as Pietro Coppo's printed map of 1524-26 (Plate 11), or Benincasa's manuscript chart of 1469 (Plate 12). Other printed maps, such as that of Martin Waldseemüller, 1513 (Plate 13), belong to a slightly different tradition which showed, in the district between England and Scotland, mountains out of which two rivers flowed, one east to the Tyne (*f[l]u tina*), the other west to a bay south of Dumfries, the mountains being topped by two 'castles', named as Newcastle and a much-confused Carlisle. It may well be that Santa Cruz, in his account, was trying to reconcile cartographic sources of these types, with which he was familiar, with his classical written sources.[129]

Santa Cruz's map, which accompanied his account, shows the Wall, without naming it, as a series of blocks. These appear (and the map has only been examined in photographs, not at first hand) to have been drawn later, over an erasure, which possibly may originally have shown that 'trench' across the island to which the account refers. At the same time, Carlisle (*carleil/lugubalia*) seems to have been added, as its portrayal is much simpler than most other towns on the map. To the north of the Wall, though, between the impressively drawn towns of Kirkudbright (*combere*) and Bamburgh (*banburgh*), he shows another, equally impressive, town called *adrianopolis*. In his text, Alonso says the place called by Ptolemy *Trimoncio* (i.e. *Trimontium* = Newstead, Roxburghshire), now has the name of *Adrianopolis*.[130] It is possible Santa Cruz had access to an

---

[128] *Islario*, 100: *una cerca o muralla* = a palisade or wall.

[129] Coppo 1524, from Shirley, plate 12: Benincasa 1469, British Library Add MS 31315 fol. 4v-5 (see also Harvey, *Medieval Maps*, plate 46): Waldseemüller 1513, private collection.

[130] *Islario*, 103.

unknown source that records an otherwise lost Roman name for a settlement here or in another part of Britian. However, in the context, Santa Cruz appears to mean that the name *Adrianopolis* is the current, that is sixteenth-century, name not a Roman name. Unfortunately, he gives no evidence or source to back up this statement; and it is difficult to avoid the conclusion that Santa Cruz had misunderstood a reference he had read somewhere concerning Hadrian's building activities in this part of Britain.

Earlier depictions of the Scottish border.

The depiction of the border between Scotland and England on early marine charts was explored in detail by Andrews in three articles published in 1926.[131] There were, going back to the fourteenth century, portolan-charts which showed Scotland either as an island or semi-island, or as separated from England by a channel, or else by a castle-crowned mountain and two rivers. Whilst it could be argued that the channel or rivers in all cases represents the Forth and Clyde, meeting at the bridge of Stirling, as shown on the Matthew Paris map, Andrews denies the possibility that Matthew Paris's maps could have influenced these marine charts, which were generally produced in Majorca or Genoa. In any case, where 'rivers and castles' are shown rather than the channel, there can be no doubt that it is the Solway-Tyne line which is meant: and charts as early as that of the Majorcan Angelino Dulcert, *c.*1339, name the castles as *castro novo* (Newcastle) and *castro berluhic* (probably from *Caer-luilid* or similar = Carlisle) (Plate 14).[132]

Andrews offers no explanation as to why the Solway-Tyne line should be shown as the Scottish border, rather than the Solway-Tweed, other than 'a confusion of thought, due to an ignorance of these northern regions'.[133] Nor does he make anything of the

---

[131] M. C. Andrews, 'Scotland in the Portolan Charts', *Scottish Geographical Magazine*, **XLII**, 1926, 129-153, 193-213: and M. C. Andrews, 'The Boundary between Scotland and England in the Portolan Charts', *Proceedings of the Society of Antiquaries of Scotland*, **LX**, 1925-26, 36-66. See also M. C. Andrews, 'The British Isles in the Nautical Charts of the XIVth and XVth Centuries', *Geographical Journal*, **LXVIII**, 1926, 474-481.

[132] Andrews, 'The Boundary between Scotland and England in the Portolan Charts', 41.

[133] Andrews, 'Boundary', 43. A reproduction of the map can be seen in plate 7, Michel Mollat du Jourdin *et al.*, *Sea Charts of the Early Explorers*, 13th to 17th Century (trans. L. le R. Dethan, London, 1984). The map itself is in the Bibliothèque Nationale, Paris: Cartes et Plans, Res. Ge B 696. The Waldseemüller map of 1513 (plate 13) is derived ultimately from this source.

30

remarkable fact that these early maps show virtually no other inland feature within Britain, and certainly give none such prominence. However, both of these difficulties could be explained by the suggestion, now put forward, that these maps may in fact have preserved a memory of a fortified line across Britain, derived from earlier, now lost, sources, which showed neither the Scottish border, nor the Forth-Clyde line, but the limits of the Roman Empire. It is highly likely that Matthew Paris had access to some late-Roman map, as a base for his work: and it is certainly possible that such a map may have incorporated that fortified line, which Matthew then incorporated into his own work. However, in the same way as Ruscelli misunderstood Lily's engraving of the Wall in 1574, so other medieval copyists with access to similar late-Roman maps could variously have interpreted different depictions of that fortified line either as 'rivers and castles', or as a channel across the island.

Indeed, it is possible that another vestige of such a map can be seen in the Cotton Anglo-Saxon map of c.1025-50 (Plate 15), a world map derived at second or third hand from a Roman source, which apparently shows Britain divided into its five late Roman provinces.[134] Although doubt has been cast by Stephen Johnson on the presence of a fifth province, the Cotton map appears to provide some evidence for its existence: however, of more importance for the present study is the sinuous line dividing *Brittannia* (sic) from *Camri* (= Cumbria, that is Strathclyde).[135] This may merely have been intended to mark the edge of the Roman world: but in the vicinity of this line appear two words which have been variously read as *march pergas, marinus portus, moren pergas* and *marin pergis.*[136]

No satisfactory explanation of any of these readings has ever been put forward. McGurk suggested it might be a seriously misplaced Gaulish place-name, *morini portus*, which seems most unlikely. Indeed, from its location on the map it is unlikely to be any *portus*, in the sense of a harbour or haven: nor does it appear to be intended

[134] British Library Cotton MS, Tiberius B.V. fol. 56v. See R. Chrone, *Early Maps of the British Isles A.D. 1000-1579* (London 1961), I, 13. The map is reproduced in colour and almost full size in P. D. A. Harvey, *Medieval Maps* (London, 1991), plate 19, and slightly larger than life in P. Barber (ed.), *The Map Book* (London, 2006), 46-47.

[135] S. Johnson, *Later Roman Britain* (St Albans, 1982, 1st published 1980), 126-7.

[136] The readings are from Chrone, 13: K. Miller, *Mappae Mundi* 1895, quoted in Chrone: P. McGurk, 'The Mappa Mundi', 79-87, in Roskilde & Bagger, *An Eleventh Century Anglo-Saxon Illustrated Miscellany* (Copenhagen, 1983), 79-87: R. V. Tooley, *Maps and Map Makers* (London, 1952), 48.

to depict a gulf or estuary, although it has been suggested it might be a much-garbled version of Ptolemy's *morikambi*.[137] Of all the readings, the meaningless *marin pergis* seems the most likely to the present writer, but there is a considerable difficulty here. The map that has come down to us has probably been copied from a copy of a Roman or post-Roman original: Beazley argued that the version we have is essentially the work of an Irish scholar monk, while McGurk saw it as a Carolingian adaptation of an earlier (Roman) map, which had been 'added to, revised, and possibly in part misunderstood in Anglo-Saxon England'.[138] What seems clear is that whatever was written in this position on the document that the eleventh-century copyist was working from meant nothing at all to him. The suggestion is now put forward that the words *marin pergis* on the Anglo-Saxon map are a bad transcription based on an attempt made by that copyist to make sense of words which themselves had been copied, and possibly misread at least once before, from a Roman original. The letter *t* in an eighth century Insular hand, for example, could easily be read as a *g* by a later scribe, and there could be similar confusion over other letters from that period. It is therefore possible that one of the versions from which the Anglo-Saxon map was ultimately derived might, just might, originally have read something like *murus pehtis* or *pictis*.

Conclusion: continuity in description and depiction

Far from disappearing from view between the time of Bede and Camden, Hadrian's Wall, as a major landscape feature, was frequently mentioned in medieval land charters. However, its significance was far more than just local, and it is clear that the Wall throughout the whole of the 800 years 'gap' remained part of the English national consciousness. The conflicting accounts of Gildas, Bede and Nennius were brought together into one coherent story, of a Severan rampart and a fifth-century stone wall: and although it could hardly be said to have dominated the chronicles in the way the Arthurian stories did, nevertheless it was as much a part of each of those chronicles as was the story of Julius Caesar or Hengist or Vortigern.

---

[137] Peter Barber, *pers com.*
[138] C. R. Beazley, *The Dawn of Modern Geography* (London, 1897), **II**, 559: McGurk, 86.

That received account of the Wall was challenged by the availability in print of 'new' classical sources, notably the *Augustan History*: but unfortunately, the first historians to have absorbed Spartianus' account, and to have accepted that Severus merely completed what Hadrian had started, were seen as being hostile to the national interests of the English, being respectively Scots and Italian. This delayed recognition of Hadrian's role, and the Wall went on being known as 'The Picts Wall' long after those historians has named it Hadrian's. Although Lhuyd and Harrison accepted it as Hadrian's, Camden seems to have been more reluctant, giving apparently equal weight to all his sources: and when in the English edition he finally accepted what he had not in the first edition, 'that the wall begun by Hadrian was finished by Severus', he could not bring himself to admit that Boece had got there first, saying instead that 'of mine opinion is Hector Boetius'.[139]

Meanwhile, many maps, from 1250 right through to the time of Camden, portrayed the Wall, thus possibly raising awareness of it amongst many who were otherwise quite oblivious to the disputes of the scholars. Indeed, the Wall's unique position as the only man-made feature, apart from the obvious towns, castles and monasteries, on these maps, must have added to perceptions of its significance as part of the national identity. Moreover, Lily's map and the later editions derived from it, together with Alonso de Santa Cruz's map, show that the Wall's fame had already moved far beyond these shores in the generations before Camden.

In addition to the surviving maps depicting Hadrian's Wall, there may have been many other manuscript maps which did so. There would certainly have been many maps, now lost, which had been copied or derived from the Paris-Gough tradition: but reference has also been made above to the possibility that portolan charts from as early as the fourteenth century, and the Cotton Anglo-Saxon map, may also retain a distant and distorted memory of the Wall, from a different tradition, ultimately derived from late-Roman maps drawn at a time when the Wall still delimited the northern end of the Roman world.

However, even if continuity of depiction for 1,600 years may be impossible to demonstrate, the idea that the Wall somehow disappeared from view between Bede and Camden, or at least between Nennius and Leland, has, hopefully, been comprehensively

[139] Camden, 1637 edn., 790.

put to rest. Leland was not the first since Bede to record an eyewitness account of the Wall: Hidgen, Hardyng and Polydore Vergil having probably all been there before him: and Ridley's is not the first mention of milecastles, Hardyng having beaten him to it by more than 100 years and possibly Vergil too, by at least 40. Finally, it is worth recording that the general adoption of the term Hadrian's Wall, which occurred only in the 1920s, was a vindication of the work of Boece, Vergil and Lhuyd, who had all decided, on the basis of their analysis of the sources, to adopt that term nearly 400 years previously. It is time they were given the recognition they deserve.

BIBLIOGRAPHY

Andrews, M. C., 'Scotland in the Portolan Charts', *Scottish Geographical Magazine*, **XLII**, 1926, 129-153, 193-213.

Andrews, M. C., 'The Boundary between Scotland and England in the Portolan Charts', *Proceedings of the Antiquaries of Scotland*, **LX**, 1925-26, 36-66.

Andrews, M. C., 'The British Isles in the Nautical Charts of the XIVth and XVth Centuries', *Geographical Journal*, **LXVIII**, 1926, 474-481.

Babington, C. (ed.), *Polychronicon Ranulphi Higden Monachi Cestriensis*, London, Rolls Series, **I-VIII**, 1865.

Bale, J., *The Laboryouse Journey & serche of Johan Leylande* (London, 1549), Preface. (Early English Books On-Line).

Barber, C., *Early Modern English* (Edinburgh, 1976).

Barber, P. (ed.), *The Map Book* (London, 2006).

Beazley, C. R., *The Dawn of Modern Geography* (London, 1897).

Birley, A., *Lives of the Later Caesars* (Harmondsworth, 1976).

Birley, E., *Research on Hadrian's Wall* (Kendal, 1961).

Blasquez, D. A. (ed.), *Islario General de Todas Las Islas del Mundo [1542]*, (Madrid, 1918).

Boece, H., *Heir beginnis the hystory and croniklis of Scotland*, 1540 (Early English Books On-Line).

Breeze, D., *J. Collingwood Bruce's Handbook to the Roman Wall, Fourteenth Edition* (Newcastle upon Tyne, 2006).

Brinley Jones, R., *Humphrey Llwyd (1527-1568)*, Oxford Dictionary of National Biography, 2004, **34**, 174-176.

Britannia, **35**, 2004, 326, 344-5.

Burton, W., *A Commentary on Antoninus, his Itinerary* (London, 1658).

Camden, G., *Britannia* (London, 1587).

Camden, W., *Britain, or a Chorographical Description of the most flourishing Kingdomes ...*, trans. P. Holland (London, 1637).

Campbell, A. (ed. & trans.), *The Chronicle of Æthelweard* (Edinburgh, 1962).

Chambers, R. W. *et al.*, *The Chronicles of Scotland, compiled by Hector Boece, Translated from the Scots by John Bellenden 1531*, Scottish Text Society, 3rd Series, **10, 15**, 1938-41.

Chrone, R., *Early Maps of the British Isles A.D. 1000-1579* (London, 1961).

Chronicorum Ethelwerdi Libri IIII (London, 1596).

Colgrave, B. & Mynors, R. A. B., *Bede's Ecclesiastical History of the English People* (Oxford, 1969).

Collingwood, R. G., 'Hadrian's Wall: A History of the Problem', *Journal of Roman Studies*, **11**, 1921, 37-66.

Connell, W. J., *Polydore Vergil, c.1470-1555*, Oxford Dictionary of National Biography, 2004, **56**, 323-327.

Core, H. O. (ed.), *Rogeri de Wendover Chronica sive Flores Historiarum* (London, English Historical Society, 1841-5).

Dahlgren, E. W., *Map of the World by Alonso de Santa Cruz* (Stockholm, 1892).

Edson, E., *Mapping Time and Space* (London, 1997).

Edwards, B. J. N., 'Raphaell Holinshed's description of Hadrian's Wall', *Hadrianic Society Bulletin*, January 1997, 7-8.

Edwards B. J. N. & Shannon W. D., 'Raphaell Holinshed's description of Hadrian's Wall', *CW3*, i, 2001, 196-201.

Ellis, H. (ed.), *The Chronicle of John Hardyng* (London, 1812).

Ellis, H. (ed.), *Polydore Vergil's English History, from an early translation preserved among the manuscripts of the old Royal Library in the British Museum* (Camden Society, 1846, Facsimile edition, Felinfach, 1996).

Fabyan, R., *The Chronicle of Fabyan* (London, 1542) (Early English Books On-Line).

Flores Historiarum per Matthaeum Westmonasteriensis (London, 1570) (Early English Books On-Line).

Forester, T. (ed. & trans.), *The Chronicle of Henry of Huntingdon* (First published 1853, facsimile reprint Felinfach, 1991).

Gilson J. P. & Poole, H., *Four maps of Great Britain designed by Matthew Paris about A.D. 1250* (London, 1928).

Given-Wilson, C., *Chronicles: The Writing of History in Medieval England* (London, 2004).

Gough, R., *British Topography, or An Historical Account of what has been done for illustrating the Topographical Antiquities of Great Britain & Ireland* (London, 1780).

Grafton, R., *The Chronicle of Jhon Hardyng* (London, 1543) (Early English Books On-Line).

Grafton, R., *Abridgement of the Chronicles of England* (London 1562) (Early English Books On-Line).

Grafton, R., *Chronicle at Large* (London 1569), (Early English Books On-Line).

Greenway, D. (ed. & trans.), *Henry, Archdeacon of Huntingdon, Historia Anglorum: The History of the English People* (Oxford, 1996).

Harvey, P. D. A., 'Matthew Paris's Maps of Britain', in P. R. Coss & S. D. Lloyd (eds.), *Thirteenth Century England*, **IV** (Woodbridge, 1991).

Harvey, P. D. A., *Medieval Maps* (London, 1991).

Hay, D. (ed. & trans.), *The Anglica Historia of Polydore Vergil A.D. 1485-1537*, Camden 3rd Series, **LXXIV**, 1950.

Haynes, H. W., 'The Roman Wall in Britain', *Journal of the American Geographical Society of New York*, **22**, 1890, 157-210.

Hearne, T., *Joannis Lelandi Antiquarii de Rebus Britannicis Collectanea* (London, 1770).

Hodgkin, T., 'The Literary History of the Roman Wall', *Archaeologia Aeliana*, **XVIII**, 2nd series, 83-108.

Ireland, S., *Roman Britain, A Sourcebook* (London, 1986).

Itinerarivm Antonini Avg (included in a collection with Pomponius Mela, Julius Solinus and other writers, Venice, in aedibus Aldi et Andreae Soceri, 1518).

Johnson, S., *Later Roman Britain* (St Alban's, 1982, 1st published 1980).

Latham, R. E., *Revised Medieval Latin Word-List* (Oxford, 1965).

Lavezzo, K., *Angels on the Edge of the World: Geography, Literature and English Community 1000-1534* (Ithaca, 2006).

Lhuyd, H., *The Breuiary of Britayne* (London 1573) (Early English Books On-Line).

Lynam, E., *The Map of the British Isles of 1546, with facsimile* (Jenkintown, 1934).

Magie, D. (trans.), *The Scriptores Historiae Augustae*, I (London, 1922).

Mattingly, H (trans.: revised by S. A. Handford), *Tacitus: The Agricola and the Germania* (Harmondsworth, 1970 edn.).

Mattingly, D., *An Imperial Possession, Britain in the Roman Empire 54 B.C.-A.D. 409* (London, 2006).

Mayer, T. F., *George Lily d.1559*, Oxford Dictionary of National Biography, 2004, **33**, 799-800.

McGurk, P., 'The Mappa Mundi' in Roskilde & Bagger, *An Eleventh Century Anglo-Saxon Illustrated Miscellany* (Copenhagen, 1983), 79-87.

Mitchell, J. B., 'The Matthew Paris Maps', *The Geographical Journal*, **81**, No 1, Jan 1933, 27-34.

Mollat du Jourdin, M., *et al.*, *Sea Charts of the Early Explorers, 13th to 17th Century* (trans. L. le R. Dethan, London, 1984).

Moore, R. W. (ed.), *The Romans in Britain: A Selection of Latin Texts with a Commentary* (London, 3rd edn. 1954, reprinted 1968).

Moreland, C. & Bannister, D., *Antique Maps* (London, 1993).

Morris, J. (ed. & trans.), *Nennius: British History and the Welsh Annals* (London, 1980).

Mynors, R. A. B., Thomson, R. M. & Winterbottom, M. (ed. & trans.), *William of Malmesbury: Gesta Regum Anglorum, History of the English Kings* (Oxford, 1998).

Parsons, E. J. S., *The Map of Great Britain circa A.D. 1360 known as the Gough Map: an introduction to the facsimile* (Oxford, 1958).

Polydori Vergilii Vrbinatis, *Anglicae Historiae Libri Vigintiseptem* (Basel, 1556).

Prescott, J. E., *The Register of the Priory of Wetherhal*, CWAAS Record Series, **I**, 1897.

Rastell, J., *The Pastyme of People* (London, 1530) (Early English Books On-Line).

Ravenhill, W., *Christopher Saxton's 16th Century maps: The Counties of England & Wales* (Shrewsbury, 1992).

Rex, R., *Robert Ridley, d.1536?*, Oxford Dictionary of National Biography, 2004, **46**, 954-955.

Rivet, A. L. F. & Smith, C., *The Place Names of Roman Britain* (London, 1981).

Roberts, P. (trans.), *The Chronicle of the Kings of Britain Translated from the Welsh copy attributed to Tysilio* (First published London, 1811: facsimile reprint Felinfach, 2000).

Robinson, M. (ed.), *The Concise Scots Dictionary* (Aberdeen, 1985).

Royan, N., *Hector Boece (c.1465-1536)*, *Oxford Dictionary of National Biography*, 2004, **6**, 418-421.

Sherley-Price, L., *Bede: A History of the English Church and People* (Harmondsworth, 1965).

Shirley, R. W., *Early Printed Maps of the British Isles 1477-1650* (East Grinstead, revised edn, 1991).

Skelton, R. A., *Saxton's Survey of England and Wales, with a facsimile of Saxton's wall-map of 1583* (Amsterdam, 1974).

Smith R. D., *William Lily 1468?-1522/3*, *Oxford Dictionary of National Biography*, 2004, **33**, 801-803.

Summerson, H., *Hardyng John, b.1377/8, d. in or after 1464*, *Oxford Dictionary of National Biography*, 2004, **25**, 240-243.

Swanton, M. (ed. & trans.), *The Anglo-Saxon Chronicle* (London, 1996).

Sweet, H., *Student's Dictionary of Anglo-Saxon* (Oxford, 1911).

Syme, R., *Ammianus and the Historia Augusta* (Oxford, 1968).

Taylor, J., *The Universal Chronicle of Ranulph Higden* (Oxford, 1966).

Thorpe, L. (ed. & trans.), *Geoffrey of Monmouth: The History of the Kings of Britain* (London, 1966).

Todd, J. (ed.) *Lanercost Cartulary*, Surtees Society, **CCIII**, and CWAAS Record Series, **XI**, 1997.

Tooley, R. V., *Maps and Map Makers* (London, 1952).

Toulmin Smith, L. (ed.), *The Itinerary of John Leland in or about the years 1535-1543* (1st edn. 1907, reprinted London, 1964).

Vaughan, R., *The Illustrated Chronicles of Matthew Paris* (Stroud, 1993).

Whitworth, A. M, *Hadrian's Wall: Some aspects of its Post-Roman Influence on the Landscape*, BAR British Series, **296**, 2000.

Winterbottom, M. (ed. & trans.), *Gildas, The Ruin of Britain and other works* (London, 1978).